P9-BIW-843

BILLY THE KID

Historical American Biographies

BILLY THE KID

Outlaw of the Wild West

Roger A. Bruns

Enslow Publishers, Inc.

40 Industrial Road   PO Box 38
Box 398   Aldershot
Berkeley Heights, NJ 07922   Hants GU12 6BP
USA   UK

http://www.enslow.com

Library of Congress Cataloging-in-Publication Data

Bruns, Roger.
    Billy the Kid : outlaw of the wild West / Roger A. Bruns.
      p. cm. — (Historical American biographies)
    Includes bibliographical references (p.) and index.
    Summary: Examines the life and illegal exploits of Billy the Kid, an
infamous bandit of the Old West.
    ISBN 0-7660-1091-0
    1. Billy, the Kid Juvenile literature. 2. Outlaws—Southwest, New
Biography Juvenile literature. 3. Frontier and pioneer life—Southwest,
New Juvenile literature. 4. Southwest, New Biography Juvenile
literature. [1. Billy, the Kid. 2. Robbers and outlaws.] I. Title. II. Series.
F786.B54B78 2000
364.15'52'092—dc21
[B]   99-16689
                                            CIP

Printed in the United States of America

10 9 8 7 6 5 4

To Our Readers: We have done our best to make sure all Internet addresses in
this book were active and appropriate when we went to press. However, the
author and the publisher have no control over and assume no liability for the
material available on those Internet sites or on other Web sites they may link to.
Any comments or suggestions can be sent by e-mail to comments@enslow.com or
to the address on the back cover.

Illustration Credits: Arizona Historical Society, pp. 12 (AHS #17658),
30 (AHS #16636), 48 (AHS #17653), 83 (AHS #17499), 92 (AHS
#17500); Courtesy, Museum of New Mexico, pp. 62 (Neg. No. 50345),
94 (Neg. No. 47640); Enslow Publishers, Inc., pp. 19, 36; Library of
Congress, pp. 17, 23, 28, 39; National Archives, pp. 6, 24, 33, 37, 76,
81; New Mexico State Records Center and Archives, p. 69; The
Museum of Modern Art, p. 105; University of Arizona Special
Collections, pp. 41, 53, 103.

Cover Illustration: National Archives (Inset); © Corel Corporation
(Background).

CONTENTS

Billy the Kid

1

THE KID ESCAPES

I'll sing you a true song of Billy the Kid,
I'll sing of the desperate deeds that he did,
Way out in New Mexico, long, long ago,
When a man's only chance was his own forty-four.

—From a folk song passed down through generations[1]

Be careful of Billy the Kid, lawmen in New Mexico said. If captured, he was extremely dangerous. No jail could hold him. His reputation as a daring, quick-thinking gunfighter, a killer with a lightning-fast draw, was well earned, they said. Some believed he had almost magical powers. Others thought he was just lucky. Could someone who looked so young and innocent be so vicious?

In April 1881, United States marshals and New Mexico authorities, led by Lincoln County Sheriff Pat Garrett, finally had Billy the Kid in custody. Convicted of murder, the Kid had been sentenced to hang.

Garrett knew that Lincoln, New Mexico, did not have a jail equipped to hold a prisoner as explosive as the Kid. He decided to hold the infamous outlaw under constant guard in the newly acquired county courthouse, a former store on the west end of town. In handcuffs and leg irons, Billy was placed in the northeast corner room. The task of guarding him was assigned to Deputy United States Marshal Bob Olinger and Deputy James W. Bell.

Described by a fellow officer as "two hundred pounds of bones and muscle," Olinger was six feet tall, with a bull neck, a huge chest, and a large head topped with shaggy hair. With bushy eyebrows, a curved, black mustache, massive arms, and fists "like hams," Olinger was a tough and mean lawman.[2]

Olinger and Billy had met before and despised each other. They had often exchanged harsh words.[3] Inside the courthouse, Olinger could not resist taunting the prisoner. Daring the Kid to try to escape, Olinger said that on hanging day, he would personally flip open the trapdoor.[4] The insults made Billy even more determined to free himself. By contrast, Bell treated Billy well.

A Risky Business

Pat Garrett had no doubt that holding Billy the Kid was risky business. One of Billy's childhood friends said later that Garrett knew that the Kid would never give up.[5]

Mrs. A. E. Lesnett, another of Billy's friends, visited the outlaw in jail. Laughing, Olinger invited Mrs. Lesnett to the hanging. Billy said to her, "Mrs. Lesnett they can't hang me if I'm not there, can they?" "Of course they can't, Billy," she said.[6]

Garrett repeatedly cautioned Olinger and Bell never to relax their guard. But Olinger continued to tease the prisoner. At one point, he said to Billy, "Just make a run for it. . . . I'd love putting a load of buckshot in your back."[7] Even Bell told Olinger to leave the Kid alone. But the cocky Olinger, enjoying his power over Billy, ignored the warning.

On April 28, with Garrett on a brief trip out of town, Billy planned his move. Bell and Olinger were responsible for five other prisoners held in another room of the courthouse. About 6:00 P.M., Olinger escorted these men across the street to the Wortley Hotel for dinner. He left his shotgun in a room in the courthouse that was used to store weapons.[8]

For a while, the Kid and Bell played cards. The Kid then asked Bell to take him to an outside toilet behind the building. As the two began to return to the room, Billy, still shackled, reached the top of the stairs before Bell and turned into the hall, out of view. Fortunately for Billy, the handcuffs did not fit securely around his small wrists and hands. Managing to slip the cuff off one wrist, he turned and swung the loose cuff at Bell, slashing his head. As Bell crumpled, the Kid leaped on him and fought to grab the officer's revolver. In the struggle, Billy succeeded in seizing the pistol, and, as Bell ran for the stairway, Billy fired. Bell tumbled down the stairs, dead.[9]

Billy got to his feet and dragged his leg irons into Garrett's office in the courthouse, where Olinger had left his loaded shotgun. Grabbing the weapon, Billy made his way to a corner room that opened onto a yard below. Resting the shotgun on the windowsill, he waited.[10]

Below, Olinger and his prisoners, alerted by the gunfire, appeared in front of the hotel. Ordering the prisoners to wait, Olinger hurried across the street.[11] A grinning Billy waited. As Olinger approached the courthouse, Billy called, "Hello, Bob." As the startled Olinger looked up, Billy opened fire.[12] Olinger crumpled, his head and upper body shredded by the buckshot he himself had packed into the twin barrels of his shotgun.

Next, the Kid went to the window at the south end of the hallway, overlooking the backyard, and shouted at Godfrey Gauss, the courthouse janitor, to bring him a pickax to break the chains. Gauss, an old friend of Billy's, willingly did what the Kid asked. With the pick, Billy severed the chain connecting his leg shackles. Looping the ends over his belt, he walked to the north end of the hall and appeared on a balcony overlooking the street. A knot of men, including the other prisoners, stood in front of the Wortley Hotel. A scattering of citizens watched silently from more distant parts of the street. None of them challenged the Kid.

Before walking down the stairs, Billy smashed the shotgun over the porch railing and hurled the pieces at Olinger's corpse.[13]

Running to Freedom

Carrying several pistols and rifles as well as the chains around his ankles, Billy had a difficult time climbing onto a black horse near the courthouse. On the first try, he was bucked off. He finally managed to get into the saddle, with both his legs on one side of the horse. With the chains slapping his legs and thighs, he rode west out of Lincoln.

Daniel Carabajal, a young boy in Lincoln at the time of Billy's escape, remembered the scene:

> I was up town playing with some boys just across the street when he killed the guards. We hid behind a picket fence and watched Billy ride out of town. We were too scared to go and see the two men that he had killed, we were afraid that he would come back and shoot us.[14]

The Lincoln County Courthouse, where Billy the Kid pulled off his dramatic escape.

Another eyewitness said that no one in Lincoln tried to bring Billy down during his escape or afterward because "they all knew he could shoot too good to risk their lives to stop him." Although many Lincoln residents filled the streets shortly after Billy's escape, they were "soon back in their homes with the doors closed until he left town."[15]

Several individuals who lived just outside Lincoln, including some farmworkers in wheat fields, remembered Billy, with his horse at a full gallop, riding sidesaddle out of town. Amelia Bolton Church, who was a young girl at the time of Billy's

A Young Boy Sees Billy the Kid

Many years after the event, a man named Sam Farner remembered the day when Billy the Kid escaped:

The day that Billy the Kid killed Bell and Olinger, my father, two brothers, and myself were irrigating our wheat field when Billy came riding by on a black horse. He stopped and hollered, "Hello Henry," Father looked up and said "Hello Billy, what are you doing here?" Billy replied, "I am going. I don't think you will see me any more. I killed two men at the Courthouse and I am on my way, good-bye." He kicked his horse and went off up the road as fast as he could.[16]

escape, later remembered, "He rode a mile and a half west before the chains were removed by a Mexican man."[17]

He was free again. When the Kid rode out of Lincoln that evening, he had added to his growing reputation as the West's most wanted outlaw.

2

WHO WAS THE KID?

Even the place of his birth has been a mystery, clouded by tall stories, myth, and a lack of hard information. Some people who knew him in the Southwest, along with some historians and western writers, have claimed that he was born in New York City in 1859. Others say that he was born in Indiana in 1861. Perhaps more than any other American historical figure, Billy the Kid's "real" life is buried in rumor and stories that have been handed down through the generations. The outlines, nevertheless, are becoming clearer.

His name was Henry, and he was the son of Catherine McCarty. He had an older brother named

Joseph. After his father and mother separated when Henry was very young, his mother and her two sons arrived in Wichita, Kansas, in 1869. She was accompanied by a friend named William Antrim, a Union Civil War veteran from Huntsville, Indiana. In Wichita, Catherine McCarty and Antrim each purchased town lots in their own names. While Antrim worked at farming and as a carpenter, Catherine McCarty ran a laundry.[1]

A Life in New Mexico

Catherine McCarty suffered from the wracking coughs and severe pain of tuberculosis. Accompanied by Antrim and her two sons, she left the Midwest and headed for New Mexico. Perhaps there, in the hot, dry climate of the desert Southwest, the good-natured Irish lady would find relief from the disease that threatened her life.[2]

In 1873, they arrived in Santa Fe, a small town in a valley surrounded by mountains. Like many other Hispanic communities in the Southwest, Santa Fe had adobe houses and buildings and a scenic plaza.[3] It looked very different from communities in the Midwest.

On March 1, soon after arriving in New Mexico, Antrim and Catherine, whose first husband had died, were married in Santa Fe.[4] Her two sons attended the wedding.[5]

Santa Fe, New Mexico, as Billy the Kid, then known as Henry McCarty, knew it.

They did not stay long in Santa Fe. Antrim and Catherine took the boys to Silver City in southwest New Mexico. There, in the foothills of a tangled web of mountains, the earth had rewarded some lucky prospectors with fortunes in gold, silver, and copper. William Antrim began to dig for a strike of his own that could make his family wealthy.

Silver City looked very different from Santa Fe. It was more like a midwestern town, with streets plotted into rectangular blocks and two-story buildings of red brick. The family moved into a log cabin on Main Street. As William Antrim searched for his strike, Catherine took in boarders at the house. Hotels and rooming houses were scarce in Silver City, and the rent from the boarders helped pay for the family's food and clothes.

About twelve years old when the family settled in Silver City, Henry was slender, with small feet and hands and a voice that gave the impression that he was even younger than his age. One of his friends later said that he probably weighed no more than seventy-five pounds. Nevertheless, Henry was never sickly. He loved to dance and sing and often played jokes on his friends and parents. Several of his friends in his primary school remarked that what he lacked in size, he made up for in great energy and quick reflexes.[6]

In the first months after the family's arrival in New Mexico, Catherine's health seemed to be

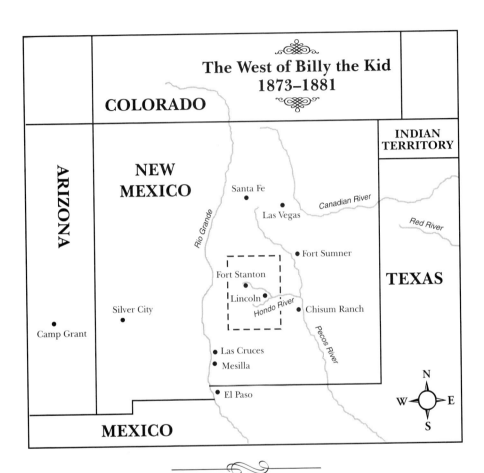

The New Mexico area where Henry McCarty Antrim first moved with his family in 1873, and where he would later become one of the most notorious outlaws in history.

improving. She often joined in the town dances held several nights a week. Catherine left a lasting impression on Henry's friends in the neighborhood. Another remembered her as a "jolly Irish lady, full of life and mischief."[7]

Unfortunately, New Mexico did not save the Antrim family. William did not find his strike. Nor did the parching winds of the New Mexico desert heal Catherine's advanced case of tuberculosis. After spending four months in bed, Catherine took her last breath at her home on September 16, 1874. She was forty-five years old.[8]

Henry and Joseph were left in the care of their stepfather. As William Antrim continued to look for the magical strike, he also took a job in a butcher shop, where Henry helped him.[9]

Later, when Antrim took a different job at a mill in a nearby town, he arranged for thirteen-year-old Henry to live with a family who had just bought a hotel. The boy waited on tables and cleaned to pay for his room and board. His brother, Joseph, stayed with a family who owned the Orleans Club, a gambling parlor and saloon. He was soon serving liquor and placing bets.[10]

Even with greater responsibilities to fend for themselves in Silver City, the two teenagers continued to go to school. Henry's teacher later remembered him as a good student with unusually clear handwriting

Life in the West

For many young boys growing up in the West, life was rugged. A man who lived his early years on a New Mexico ranch remembered: "Father provided a shack for the family to live in, near the ranch. The only things I saw while growing up were critters, cowhands, and wild animals."[11]

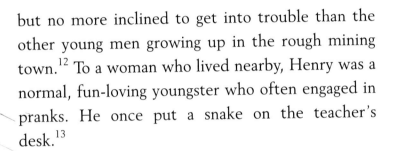

but no more inclined to get into trouble than the other young men growing up in the rough mining town.[12] To a woman who lived nearby, Henry was a normal, fun-loving youngster who often engaged in pranks. He once put a snake on the teacher's desk.[13]

In the Midst of Violence

Mining towns such as Silver City were rough places. Killings, knifings, and drunken brawls were commonplace. One visitor, upon riding into New Mexico for the first time, wrote, "All the men have a great 'six-shooter' slung on their hip, & a knife on the other. . . ." Everyone went about their business, he said, prepared for trouble.[14]

Henry found trouble at an early age. He joined a gang of youngsters whom a Silver City newspaper editor called "The Village Arabs." He took to gambling. Like his brother, he began to deal poker and

monte, the most popular card games. He became a first-class card player, according to one of his friends.[15]

In September 1875, a newspaper in New Mexico reported the news that Henry had been arrested for stealing some shirts off a clothesline at a Chinese laundry in Silver City. A local newspaper reported, "It's believed that Henry was simply the tool of 'Sombrero Jack,' who done the stealing whilst Henry done the hiding."[16] Although, as the newspaper suggested, it is likely that Henry's friend, George "Sombrero Jack" Shaffer had committed the actual theft and that Henry was only an accomplice, the local sheriff decided to teach Henry a lesson. He was placed in a cramped cell in the town's old jail.[17]

The teenager proved to be more wily than his captors. Complaining that the long hours in the cell had caused his legs to cramp, he asked permission to exercise in the outer room. When the guard left the room for a brief moment, Henry climbed up the chimney and escaped to the street below.[18] A resident of Silver City said, "The Kid was a slim boy who could always get a laugh from any source whether the joke being on him or someone else . . . the boy was able by some means to climb through the chimney.[19]

Grabbing a horse, Henry rode out of town, heading west. It is likely he saw his stepfather and that

The violence and gunplay of the West was often depicted in the
National Police Gazette.

Billy the Kid became an expert gambler and especially liked the game of faro. This is a card game under way in Arizona.

Antrim gave him some money. Antrim probably also gave the boy advice to head to Arizona. In late September 1875, Henry caught a stagecoach in Silver City and rode to Globe, Arizona. It was approximately a year after his mother's death. He was about fourteen years old.[20]

The whole incident in Silver City had been something of a mistake. The sheriff had intended to scare the boy, keep him in jail for a couple of days, and then let him go. The boy was more acrobatic and resourceful than the jailer would have imagined. The jail did not hold the Kid. No jail would ever hold him for very long.

After he arrived in Arizona, Henry McCarty took the last name of Antrim after his stepfather. At other times, to avoid capture, the boy began to use various other names. He became "Billy" and sometimes used "Bonney" as his last name. Although never proven, the name was perhaps the last name of his real father. From these early days in Arizona throughout the rest of his life, however, whether he went by the name of Henry McCarty, William Bonney, or William Antrim, he was always known as the Kid, or Billy the Kid.[21]

3

THE KID NOTCHES HIS FIRST

In the San Simeon Valley of Arizona, there were plenty of amusements to attract a young boy like Billy. In towns such as Safford and Pueblo, there were rowdy and wild saloons, dance halls, and gambling parlors. They lit up the Arizona nights for the young cowboys who herded cattle on farms and ranches along the Gila River. The typical trail hand was described by a newspaperman in 1871:

> . . . the occupation of his heart is gambling. His dress consists of a flannel shirt with a handkerchief encircling his neck . . . his head is covered with a sombrero, which is a Mexican hat with a low crown and a brim of mammoth dimensions. He generally wears a revolver on each side, which he will use with as little hesitation on a man as on a wild animal.[1]

As settlers moved in, new dance houses cropped up across the West. Billy the Kid became a skilled dancer.

For a time, young Billy became one of those cowboys. "He came to my camp at Fort Thomas and asked for work," said W. J. "Sorghum" Smith, who ran a hay farm in Pima County. Billy said he was seventeen, Smith remembered, although he did not look older than fourteen.[2]

Billy later took a job at Camp Grant, a cavalry post at the foot of majestic Mount Graham. Working as a teamster, he drove log teams from a timber forest to Camp Grant's sawmill.[3] He also worked at the nearby Sierra Bonita Ranch, handling wagon teams and roping steers.

The "Cowboy Hat"
In western movies, cowboys often wore "ten-gallon" hats—large, extravagant, and, in the case of Hollywood heroes, usually white. In fact, most real western cowboys wore Mexican-style hats with enormous brims that gave shade under the intense sun. Hats were part of the cowboy's practical work uniform.

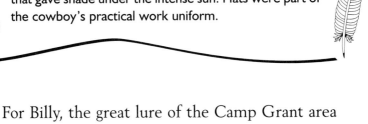

For Billy, the great lure of the Camp Grant area was the gambling tables. "Gambling and drinking saloons and dance houses were numerous," remembered one of the men at Camp Grant. Billy became so skilled as a card player that he began to work as a dealer at Atkins's saloon.[4]

Rustling

These brief encounters with legitimate work did not satisfy the restless Billy. He began hanging out with a gang of rustlers. In early 1877, the gang stole three horses near the headquarters of the Norton & Stewart Cattle Company. The horses were not the property of the cattle company; they belonged to some soldiers stationed at Camp Thomas. Billy and his friends now had members of the United States Army on their trail.

In late March 1877, Billy was captured and placed in the guardhouse at Camp Grant. Like the

Billy the Kid often had lawmen looking for him. These men are
Arizona Rangers of the time.

jailer in New Mexico, the army soon found out that
Billy was not an easy individual to confine. The boy
escaped on the same day he was jailed.[5]

In the spring and summer of 1877, Billy was
arrested two more times. And two more times he
escaped, once by squeezing through a small opening
in the roof of a guardhouse.[6]

Blue-eyed, short, and strong in the shoulders, Billy
was also bright and energetic. One of his acquaintances said he strutted around with a six-gun stuffed
in his trousers.[7] Another friend thought he was like
a cat, graceful and quick. He continually practiced

with a rifle and could shoot a pistol with either hand. He also had very small wrists.[8] He could often slip out of handcuffs.

He learned to speak Spanish and always had many friends among the Hispanic people in New Mexico and across the Mexican border. One of the farmers living in Lincoln, New Mexico, said, "he was always nice to the Spanish people and they all liked him."[9] One of his Hispanic friends said that Billy was "Siempre muy caballero" (always very much a gentleman).[10]

Death of the Blacksmith

In the rough, frontier towns of the West, violent men often met violent ends. During a card game in a Camp Grant saloon in August 1877, Billy joined that world of violence.

One of the card players was a large blacksmith named Frank Cahill, a man who had a history of badgering and slapping around youngsters such as Billy. The blacksmith was nicknamed "Windy" because of his tough-talking, threatening manner. Gus Gildea, a cowboy who frequented the bar, remembered Cahill throwing Billy down on the bar-room floor and slapping him in front of the other cowboys. According to Gildea, the blacksmith would "slap his [Billy's] face and humiliate him before the men in the saloon."[11]

On August 17, Windy Cahill badgered the Kid for the last time. Windy threw Billy down, pinned his arms, and once again began slapping him. The teenager's right arm was free from the elbow down. He worked his arm around, grabbed his gun, stuck the barrel into the blacksmith's stomach, and fired. Cahill died from the wound. One witness said of Billy's act, "He had no choice; he had to use his equalizer."[12] Although several other observers said that the Kid had clearly acted in self-defense, a local jury determined that the shooting was "criminal and unjustified."[13]

On the following morning, a justice of the peace arrested Billy as he was eating breakfast at a hotel and jailed him in the guardhouse at Camp Grant. As he had done many times before, Billy did not stay in jail for long. He again escaped, stole a horse; and rode east.[14]

Now he was a fugitive fleeing a murder conviction. With Arizona lawmen now on his trail, he told one rancher that he was thinking of going back to New Mexico. For Billy, Arizona was no longer a safe place.[15]

At a ranch about forty miles south of Silver City, New Mexico, where he had some friends, Billy stayed for a few days and then continued heading east. Afraid of moving along well-traveled trails, he rode through the Guadalupe Mountains to the

The law did not look like much in parts of Arizona when Billy the Kid was there. This is one of the jails.

Pecos Valley along an old American Indian trail. Along the way, he lost his horse and nearly lost his life.

Spotted by members of an Apache tribe who began to close in on him, Billy managed to hide along a creek bed. Exhausted and out of food, he showed up on foot at a ranch owned by a man named Heiskell Jones and his wife, Barbara. The family nursed him back to health.[16]

In the wild atmosphere of the West, Billy had become an adult. He had worked, gambled, and killed. A friend later said, "Billy preferred adventure."[17]

4

A WAR
BREWING IN
LINCOLN
COUNTY

Nestled in a beautiful valley on the banks of the Rio Bonito (Pretty River), Lincoln County, New Mexico, played an important part in the heritage of the Southwest. Apache had dominated this part of the territory for at least three hundred years. Fine hunters and fierce warriors, the Apache resisted Hispanic settlers who increasingly moved into the area in the middle of the nineteenth century. As the Hispanics built several small villages along the Rio Bonito, Apache tribes waged aggressive war against them. Nevertheless, the settlements continued.

Settlers from the eastern United States also moved into the territory. They came first by wagon

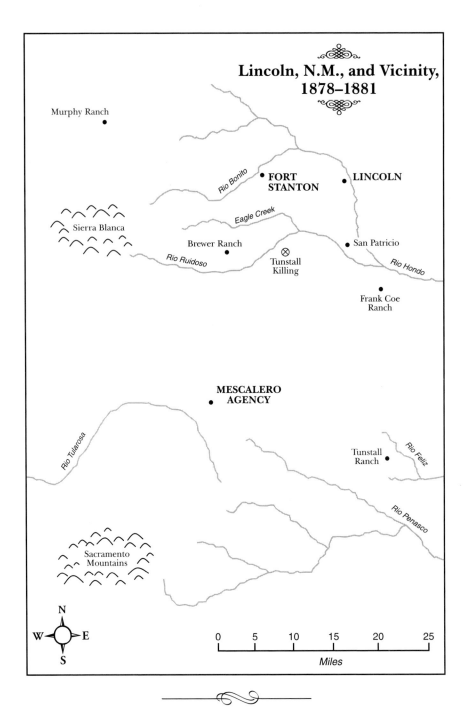

Lincoln, N.M., and Vicinity, 1878–1881

Murphy Ranch

Rio Bonito

FORT STANTON

LINCOLN

Eagle Creek

Sierra Blanca

Brewer Ranch

Rio Ruidoso

⊗ Tunstall Killing

San Patricio

Rio Hondo

Frank Coe Ranch

MESCALERO AGENCY

Rio Tularosa

Tunstall Ranch

Rio Feliz

Rio Penasco

Sacramento Mountains

N
W · E
S

| 0 | 5 | 10 | 15 | 20 | 25 |

Miles

Lincoln County, New Mexico, would become the scene of a violent war between different cattle interests in which Billy the Kid would play a role.

and then by the newly built railroad. As increasing numbers of settlers arrived, the United States Army, to maintain order, established Fort Stanton in 1855. The soldiers were soon busy herding the Apache onto a nearby reservation.

The government needed large quantities of beef to supply Fort Stanton and to fill the ration requirements of the Indians. Cattlemen from Texas arrived to take advantage of the growing market. It was to this area that Billy the Kid moved and built his reputation.[1]

When Billy arrived in Lincoln, he saw several dozen flat-roofed adobe buildings strung along a main dirt street. He entered a town of less than a

The rugged desert around Fort Stanton, New Mexico, where Billy the Kid spent many days.

thousand residents, mostly Hispanic. The most unusual sight in the town was a two-story _torreón_, or "round tower," a twenty-foot stone fortress erected many years earlier by the residents for defense against attacks by American Indian tribes.[2]

The Fugitive and the Lincoln County Mess

Billy was a teenage drifter when he rode into Lincoln in October 1877, a fugitive from the Arizona murder charge. For a few months, he worked at a ranch owned by Frank Coe and his cousin, George. Billy and George Coe hunted wild game in the mountains and sold some of the meat to Fort Stanton. Frank Coe said later that Billy spent much of his spare time cleaning his six-shooter and target practicing: "He could take two six-shooters, loaded and cocked, one in each hand . . . and twirl one in one direction and the other in the other direction, at the same time."[3]

By the fall of 1877, Billy had signed on as a cowhand at the ranch of John H. Tunstall. In doing so, the Kid plunged himself into the middle of a conflict that soon became known as the Lincoln County War.[4]

The struggle was for control of the beef industry in New Mexico. Louis Bousman, who worked for another of the cattlemen in Lincoln County, described the conflict in simple terms: "It was a

For a time, Billy the Kid worked on ranches, busting broncos like this western cowboy.

cowman's war. They were fighting over the grazing land for the cattle."[5]

On the one side of the fight was the company owned by Lawrence G. Murphy. A former divinity student from Ireland and soldier in the United States Army, Murphy became the post trader at Fort Stanton. His questionable business dealings got him fired by the post commander. Murphy then moved to Lincoln and built an organization that gained a monopoly on supplying beef and flour to Fort Stanton. Some of the beef sold by Murphy to

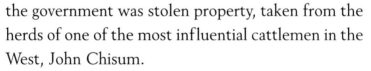

The Cattle Industry
The first cattle came to America with Christopher Columbus on his second voyage in 1494. Thriving on the rich grasslands of the Caribbean and Mexico, herds of cattle were taken north, and organized ranching first appeared in the American Southwest around 1600. By the time of Billy the Kid, the cattle industry was thriving in New Mexico and Texas and other parts of the Southwest as ranchers drove massive herds to railroad lines to be shipped to the crowded cities in the East.

the government was stolen property, taken from the herds of one of the most influential cattlemen in the West, John Chisum.

In the tall grass plains of eastern New Mexico and western Texas, John Chisum's herds of cattle, nearly one hundred thousand head, ranged along the Pecos River. Leathery-faced, rugged, and a shrewd businessman, Chisum knew the cow business as few others did, and protected it with a formidable group of gunslingers.

Although his gunmen attacked Murphy's cattle thieves, who were preying on his herds, Chisum did not succeed in eliminating Murphy's business. Indeed, Murphy thrived. Ruthless and shrewd, Murphy was able to make himself the cattle king of Lincoln County.[6]

The New Mexico ranch house of John Chisum, one of the country's most powerful cattle barons.

On the other side in the cattle war in Lincoln was John Tunstall, the twenty-three-year-old son of a prominent merchant in London, England. At age eighteen, the young Tunstall had traveled to America in search of fortune. He spent two years in Canada, working in a branch of his father's mercantile business, but found it dull and depressing. After spending time in California, he had come to the rugged New Mexico ranching country with dreams of establishing a cattle empire.[7] Nevertheless, Tunstall sensed the dangers that life in New Mexico held. He told his parents that it was "about the toughest little spot in America."[8]

Tunstall opened a store and a bank, purchased a ranch in Lincoln, and hired, among others, Billy the Kid. Billy became very fond of his new boss. Billy's friend Frank Coe later remembered that when Tunstall hired the Kid, he made him "a present of a good horse and a nice saddle and a new gun. My, but the boy was proud—said it was the first time in his life he had ever had anything given to him."[9]

In challenging the interests of the Murphy Company, Tunstall did not fully realize how ruthlessly Murphy ruled Lincoln. Murphy's hired gunmen patrolled Lincoln County like a small army. Even the sheriff, William Brady, was a close ally of Murphy's.[10]

Tunstall's equally ambitious older partner was an asthmatic Canadian lawyer named Alexander A.

McSween. A man of books and learning, McSween seemed out of place in a raw frontier place such as Lincoln County. Born of Scottish parents, McSween had once been a Presbyterian clergyman and had later studied law at Washington University in St. Louis. When McSween, with his sweeping handlebar mustache, and his attractive, well-dressed wife, Susan, arrived in Lincoln, they attracted much attention.[11]

Tunstall and McSween quickly became friends and partners. The two formed a business alliance, determined to control most of the wealth of the cattle industry in Lincoln County. To accomplish that feat, Tunstall's enterprise had to oust the Murphy Company from control of the area's beef interests. In that daring move were planted the seeds of a violent conflict.

From the time Tunstall's intentions to challenge the Murphy Company became known, rumors swirled through Lincoln County about the possibility of assassination attempts on Tunstall's life. Knowing that his business ventures could erupt into violence and that his own life was in jeopardy, Tunstall brought in some new ranch hands whose skill at handling Winchester rifles, pistols, and knives was as good or better than their ability to handle steers. The small army, Tunstall told his relatives, had cost him a lot of money.[12]

If Lawrence Murphy ruled as a ruthless business king, he was, at the same time, succumbing to the ravages of alcoholism. One of his acquaintances said that Murphy could no longer run the business. All he could do, said the friend, was drink whiskey.[13]

As the disease took its toll on Murphy, he turned his business over to a junior partner, James J. Dolan. Dolan soon bought out the business and renamed it J. J. Dolan & Company. Under Dolan, the company continued to intimidate ranchers and farmers and continued to deal in stolen cattle.

Dolan's boys were ready to take out their competitor—brutally and violently.[14]

The Murder of John Tunstall

The trouble in New Mexico came to a head on a cold night in February 1878. In a wooded canyon near Ruidoso, as he was driving nine horses toward the town of Lincoln with several of his ranch hands, including Billy, Tunstall was temporarily separated on the trail from the others. As he waited for them to return, he was shot twice and killed by Dolan's hired gunmen. The killers included Jesse Evans and Andrew Roberts, a former Texas Ranger. A veteran of many gunfights, Roberts had been shot numerous times and still carried in his body so many bullets that he was nicknamed "Buckshot."[15] By killing John Tunstall, Evans, Buckshot Roberts, and the others had elevated the rivalry between the two sides in New Mexico to new levels.

The killing of Tunstall sparked the beginning of the Lincoln County War. Berta Ballard Manning, a woman who grew up in Lincoln County during the wild times, later said: "I don't see how my mother ever stood the excitement and anxiety of those wild lawless days. Of course, we children didn't realize the danger of the outlaws shootings . . . that kept the old town of Lincoln in a constant turmoil."[16]

Back in Lincoln, as Billy stood over the fresh grave of his friend John Tunstall, he vowed that he would never stop until he had killed every man involved in Tunstall's murder.[17] Embittered, thirsting for revenge, Tunstall's men would soon be ready to go after the murderers.

5

THE REGULATORS

They called themselves "The Lincoln County Regulators." They were Tunstall men—local cowboys, ranchers, and gunslingers who had worked for Tunstall or had become his allies. They were now out to avenge his death. John Tunstall's ranch hands were about to become executioners.

The Regulators were organized by Tunstall's foreman, Dick Brewer. Tall and handsome, Brewer was a fine horseman and a deadly shot. In early March 1878, Brewer and his men tracked down two of the men who had murdered Tunstall. At a site later called Dead Man's Draw, the Regulators killed the two men. The scene was gruesome. Each of the victims was shot eleven times, apparently one time for each of the Regulators at the scene. The viciousness of the act underscored the deep hatred between the two sides in the escalating conflict in Lincoln County. The next victim would be Sheriff William Brady.[1]

Assassination

Brady had become sheriff of Lincoln County when it was first organized in 1869. He was openly on the side of the Murphy-Dolan Company, deeply involved in many of their schemes, and, some people believed, on their payroll. He had been a fierce

Main Street in Lincoln, New Mexico, as it looked during the days of Billy the Kid.

enemy of Tunstall, and members of his posse were responsible for Tunstall's murder.

On the morning of April 1, 1878, in a corral behind Tunstall's Lincoln store, Billy the Kid and some companions waited in ambush to kill Brady. About nine o'clock in the morning, as Brady and several deputies walked down the street toward the Lincoln courthouse, Billy and the others rose from behind a wall, leveled their Winchester rifles, and opened fire. Torn apart by a dozen bullets, Brady crumpled dead in the middle of the street; beside him lay the body of one of his deputies. The other deputies managed to scramble to safety in a house across the street.[2]

Amelia Bolton Church, a prominent resident of Lincoln, recalled the killing of Brady and his deputy: "I saw him as he and another man, deputy sheriff George Hindman, lay dead in the street, shot down, as they were, by Billy the Kid and his gang, who lay hidden behind an adobe wall. . . . Brady was killed instantly."[3]

The deputies fought back. From a shower of gunfire erupting from one of the houses, Billy took a bullet in one of his thighs. He managed to get to his horse and rode with the Regulators out of town. With this killing—a cold-blooded murder in the middle of town—they had struck the latest and most open act of warfare in the Lincoln County War.[4]

Shootout at Blazer's Mill

A few days later, west of Lincoln, about five of the Regulators arrived at a place called Blazer's Mill, named after Dr. Joseph Blazer, who ran a sawmill there. A friend of several of the Regulators, Blazer informed the men that Buckshot Roberts, one of the men involved in John Tunstall's killing, was also there at Blazer's Mill. Unfortunately for Roberts, he was there alone.

If the Regulators thought they had an easy prey, however, they underestimated Buckshot Roberts. Blazer's Mill became the site of a bloody shootout— Buckshot Roberts versus several of the Regulators. In defending himself against the Regulators, Roberts became something of a one-man army. Though shot through the stomach early in the fight, Roberts made a stand at a doorway, firing his Winchester rifle from the hip. When Billy rushed him, the Kid was slammed in the stomach by the butt of the rifle. The wounded Roberts retreated to an inside room, barricaded the door, used a mattress as a shield, and waited.

For several minutes, there was silence. Dick Brewer, the Regulator leader, wondering why Roberts had not shot, peeked up over the woodpile. It was the last thing he ever did. Roberts fired and Brewer fell, the top of his head shot off. Another of the Regulators lost his thumb in the fight. It was

Legendary "Dead Shots"

Tales of fast-drawing, dead-eye gunslingers have filled novels and movie screens. The great gunfighter Wild Bill Hickok, it was said, once drew two revolvers, spun each of them, cocked, and fired repeatedly at a tin can he kept jumping for an entire city block. Pat Garrett once said, however, that hitting a one-and-a-half-inch bull's-eye twice out of five shots at fifteen paces would be "very good shooting."[5]

taken off as cleanly as if a surgeon had removed it, said one of the residents of Lincoln. One of Roberts's bullets took a nick out of Billy's shirt.[6] One of the Regulators said later that Roberts handled a Winchester rifle as fast as any man he ever saw.[7]

Buckshot Roberts was never ousted from the room. After suffering several casualties from the gun of the plucky warrior, the Regulators decided to leave him in the room to die from his wound. He lasted until the next morning. With the deaths of Roberts and Dick Brewer, the Lincoln County War had claimed two more victims. It would claim many others.[8]

An Odd Mix

To many who knew Billy the Kid during these days, he was an odd mix of young boy and artful killer.

Billy lived for several months at the McSween ranch. Francisco Gomez, one of the workers at the ranch, described Billy as "an awfully nice young fellow with light brown hair, blue eyes, and rather big front teeth. He always dressed very neatly."[9]

José Montoya, a youngster of about eleven years old who knew the Kid in Lincoln, said that Billy was very popular with the Hispanic community around Lincoln County.[10] He learned to speak Spanish very well among the sheepherders, played marbles with their children, and seemed to make friends everywhere he went.[11]

One rancher reported that members of the Hispanic community often hid the Kid under the floors of their houses and protected him in other ways.[12] A number of individuals later remembered that Billy had become close friends with a number of Hispanic girls.[13] He often attended weekly dances in Lincoln. One young woman remembered Billy as "a gallant figure at these affairs. He was not handsome, but he had a certain sort of boyish good looks. He was always smiling and good-natured and very polite and danced remarkably well, and the little Mexican beauties made eyes at him."[14] Throughout eastern New Mexico and into the Texas Panhandle, Billy struck up relationships with several women. One of them gave birth to a daughter. It was commonly believed in the Lincoln area that the girl had been fathered by Billy.[15]

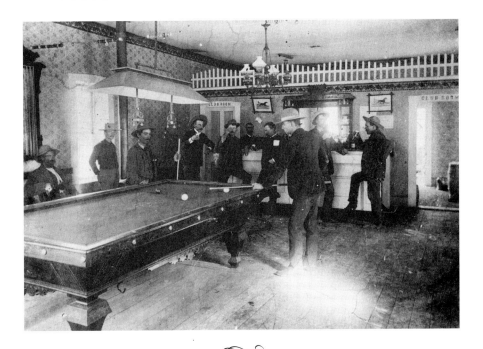

A pool room in Lincoln, New Mexico, in the 1880s.

Mrs. A. E. Lesnett, who ran a general store and hotel in Lincoln, remembered that Billy often played games with her two children:

He was very fond of children, and liked Irvin and Jennie Mae at once. . . . [H]e would take the two of them for a ride on his gray pony. He also had a little dog which was very spirited. . . . [H]e would laughingly pull his gun and begin firing into the ground, the dog would playfully follow every puff of dust, yelping joyfully.[16]

The Kid was a fast and expert marksman. "He used to practice target shooting a lot," Francisco

Gomez said. "He would throw up a can and would twirl his six gun on his finger and he could hit the can six times before it hit the ground."[17]

Another young boy of one of the ranches said,

> Whenever I met him he acted mighty decent and 'twas generally said about him that he never turned a fellow down that was up against it and called for a little help. But, also, the folks allowed he would shoot a man just to see the fellow give the dying kick. 'Twas said he got a powerful lot of amusement out of watching a fellow, that he didn't like, twist and groan.[18]

Charlie Ballard, one of Billy's friends in Lincoln, said,

> He was small for a youth of his age. He weighed only about a hundred and twenty-five or thirty pounds, and was quick and active as a cat. He was a very fine rider. We often rode and raced our ponies together. . . . I am one of the many who appreciated his good qualities in spite of his career as a two-gunman and killer.[19]

A Campaign of Violence

With Billy taking an increasing leadership role, the Regulators ambushed and murdered Tunstall's opponents, battled lawmen who got in their way, and terrorized much of the community.[20] The Lincoln County War was becoming a war not only among armed men but also for the loyalty of the citizens of the state. A woman who lived in Lincoln County during the war later said,

Many unknown graves dot the surrounding country and many human bones lie bleaching in the sun for they carried on guerrilla warfare. When one party met the other while riding through the hills they just opened fire, either pushing forward or retreating . . . if all the men were accounted for their graves might reach from Roswell to White Oaks.[21]

6

THE BATTLE OF LINCOLN

Beginning on July 15, 1878, Lincoln became the scene of a standoff between competing mini-armies of gunslingers, cowboys, United States soldiers, outlaws, lawmen, and assorted private citizens. The hired thugs of the two sides in the Lincoln County War, who were holed up in various buildings, including the *torreón*—the old stone fortress—turned the town into a combat zone. For a few sweltering summer days, the Lincoln County War turned from a series of murders and assassinations into a full-scale battle between massed groups of fighters. The conflict was becoming one of the most bizarre spectacles in the history of the American West.

The battle began when Sheriff George "Dad" Peppin of Lincoln, an open supporter of the Murphy-Dolan side, decided the time had come for a showdown. Determined to end the menace of the Regulators once and for all, the sheriff gathered a little army of about forty men into the Wortley Hotel, just down the street from the McSween House. McSween and his own little army of Regulators spread out in several locations in the town, prepared for battle. They brought to the battle a force of nearly sixty fighters. A dozen or more were first-rate gunmen such as Billy.

Sheriff Peppin's posse, although fewer in number than the Regulators, included numerous professional gunmen. It also had behind it the authority of Peppin's badge, and arrest warrants for various members of the Regulators from several federal and territorial courts. Peppin's posse saw itself as the law-and-order side and expected that in any lengthy confrontation, it might be assisted by soldiers from nearby Fort Stanton.[1] Both sides, of course, counted God on their side.

For the next several days, Lincoln became an almost silly, if not tragic, scene of threats, counter-threats, insults, sniper fire, and assorted military maneuvers. Positioned behind walls, at windows, and rooftops, men shot up the town, killed numerous animals, and occasionally wounded each other.

Some combatants even carted around a cannon and a Gatling gun.

What to Do With the Army?

With bullets whizzing about in all directions, many citizens spent hours huddled on the floors of their homes and stores. A few concerned individuals managed to leave their houses and head to the fort to try to talk the commanding officer, Colonel Nathan Dudley, into intervening. Although Dudley had received strict orders from his army commanders to be neutral in the conflict, he became increasingly disturbed by the threat being imposed upon the citizens of the city. Early on the evening of July 18, Dudley had heard enough. The danger to women and children was such, he concluded, that the town of Lincoln needed the presence of the United States Army.

On July 19, Dudley brought about forty soldiers into Lincoln. As Billy and his friends looked out from the McSween House, Colonel Dudley, to the blaring sound of bugles, led his blue column of men down the street—four officers, followed by eleven mounted black troopers of the 9th Cavalry and twenty-four white footmen of the 15th Infantry. At the rear of the column, pulled along by some infantrymen, rolled a small twelve-pound mountain howitzer, a medium-range cannon. Billy and others

thought Dudley had come to wipe out the Regulators.

Colonel Dudley soon informed everyone that he had come solely to protect women and children and would not take sides. If either side endangered his camp, he said, he would respond with force. This show of neutrality, he thought, might persuade the two sides to come to peaceable terms.[2] It did not work out that way.

The arrival of the military frightened many of the Regulators outside the McSween residence. Concluding that Dudley had decided to join Peppin and that they would soon face cannon blasts, many of McSween's men left the scene. Billy and others were now mostly concentrated in one central location, Alexander McSween's residence. Colonel Dudley's actions had placed the Regulators in great jeopardy.

Billy the Kid and the other men inside McSween's house now began to wait it out. Both sides continued heavy firing, but the battle was a standoff. Early in the afternoon, McSween's wife, Susan, decided that she would talk to Dudley. As she walked out of the McSween residence, no gunfire greeted her appearance. When she headed toward the military troops, however, she saw what the opposition had in mind. They had decided to burn down the McSween House.

Burning out the Regulators

At the *torreón*, Susan McSween argued hotly with Sheriff Peppin, who told her that if she wanted to save her house from flames, she had to persuade the men inside to surrender. At the military camp, she screamed at Dudley to prevent the destruction of her family's home. Dudley stubbornly refused to interfere in any way with a sheriff in the lawful discharge of his duty. Susan McSween returned to the house. When the men inside the house realized they were about to be burned out, they persuaded her to leave.[3]

The anti-McSween forces went to work. They soaked a barrel with coal-oil and rolled it down the hill toward the McSween House. The strategy worked. Although the outside of the house was made of adobe, there was much wood and other flammable material to catch fire inside. The house began to burn slowly, first one room and then another. The occupants, approximately fourteen of them, were in grave danger.

Knowing that he and the other men were in desperate straits, Billy told them to prepare for a breakout. The only chance for escape was to run across a thirty-foot space behind the house, roll under a fence, and follow the bed of the Rio Bonito to safety. The flames showered the night sky with light but the space behind the building lay in shadows.

Susan McSween played a critical role in the Lincoln County War.

Perhaps they could make it across before being spotted by the posse. With the flames devouring the house foot by foot and lighting up the hills on both sides of the town, the men retreated to the last untouched room. The attempted breakout came shortly after 9:00 P.M. One by one, the men slipped out the door into the yard and crept toward the fence in single file.[4]

Not until the men were in the middle of the space between the fence and the building did the light of the flames fall on them. Suddenly, bullets were streaming toward the men from both sides of the house. Several of the men made it to the fence, crawled under, and lost themselves in the darkness of the river and its sheltering trees.[5]

When Billy ran from the house, someone yelled, "Here comes the Kid!" With bullets whizzing by his head, snapping at his feet, and raising dust all around him, he streaked across the space, dodging from side to side. Several shots hit his clothes and hat; none hit his body. He made it to the fence, rolled under it, and scrambled down to the river, the bullets still filling the air.[6]

The remaining men gathered at the back door. One by one they tried to cross the thirty-foot distance and one by one they fell. Alexander McSween himself was shot down at the door.[7] A maze of bullets had sprayed from all sides, ricocheting off the

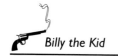

ground and off the house. The lawyer had been hit with nine bullets.[8]

With several bodies strewn about McSween's backyard, including the body of McSween himself, Sheriff Peppin's posse gloated over its victory. With several killed and wounded and the others on the run, the Regulators were a broken army. The Battle of Lincoln was over.

The Aftermath of Battle

The widowed Susan McSween later hired an attorney to sue the federal government for not protecting her husband and her property. She planned to direct the suit against Colonel Dudley, whose troops in Lincoln had allowed the battle to proceed and had allowed her house to burn down. Susan McSween's lawyer, however, had taken on his last case. He was murdered in the street by Dolan's men.[9]

Lawrence G. Murphy did not play a part in the Battle of Lincoln. After selling his interest in the business to his partners and being threatened with death by the Regulators, he had fled to Fort Stanton. His continuing bout with alcoholism resulted in his death in a Santa Fe hospital just before the Battle of Lincoln began.[10]

The escape from McSween's blazing home gave Billy some attention in the area newspapers. As yet, however, he was simply one of about a dozen

Regulators whose names appeared in the papers whenever they fought a skirmish or shot a member of the opposition. But the five-day battle gave Billy a taste of gunfire in truly frightening proportions. Trapped in a situation that seemed hopeless, he had kept his head.

One of the farmers' wives in Lincoln said later, "I remember the day the McSween home was burned. We could see the flames and smoke from our house but we stayed at home for we were scared to death to stick our heads out of the house. We could also hear some of the shooting."[11]

Another eyewitness remembered accompanying Susan McSween to her burned-out house the next day: "We found only the springs and other wires of her piano that was the pride of her life. She raked in the ashes where her bureau had stood and found her locket."[12]

From this five-day struggle came stories and tall tales that would add to the legend of one of the anti-Murphy-Dolan leaders who escaped—Billy the Kid.

The Lincoln County War should have ended after the Battle of Lincoln. The war itself had been about economic power—Murphy-Dolan against Tunstall-McSween. By the time the citizens of Lincoln buried the bodies of the men who fell in McSween's back-yard, the economic struggle was, indeed, over. Tunstall and McSween were both dead. The Dolan

Company was so severely hurt by the war that it was bankrupt. Nevertheless, the war did not end. Too much hatred and division had smoldered in Lincoln for too long. The remaining participants on both sides wanted revenge, and they wanted total victory. The war kept its own momentum, regardless of who was left to fight and regardless of the reasons it had started in the first place.

The victors of the Battle of Lincoln, the mini-army that had torched McSween's house and killed many of the men inside, now rushed around the New Mexico countryside as if suddenly freed of all restraints from the remaining Regulators or from the law itself. Many of them stole cattle belonging to supporters of Tunstall and McSween. They maimed and killed men, broke into and looted houses, burned buildings, and, in a few cases, attacked women. At a farm owned by an Hispanic family who had been friendly to Tunstall, they rode up to three men cutting hay and shot them all dead without asking questions. At another ranch, they asked a teenage boy to fetch some watermelons. After he did as they asked, they killed him. One citizen observed that large groups of people had left their homes and fled to safety. Tragically, Lincoln County seemed to be totally without law enforcement. New Mexico needed leadership.[13]

7

RUNNIN' AND RUSTLIN'

Even though isolated in New Mexico, the Lincoln County War had become national news. In Washington, D.C., President Rutherford B. Hayes ordered the Justice Department to investigate the violence. The report convinced the president that a new governor, with United States Army troops, should take over New Mexico to bring the Lincoln County mess under control. President Hayes selected General Lew Wallace of Indiana to do the job.[1]

General Wallace to the Rescue

Fifty-one years old with a modest law practice in Crawfordsville, Indiana, Wallace had risen through

the military ranks during the Mexican War and had become a Union general during the Civil War. At the Battle of Shiloh, General Ulysses S. Grant had criticized Wallace for failing to get his division on the battlefield promptly. Grant's critical appraisal of Wallace's leadership qualities dampened the Indiana soldier's career in the military. Bitter and defiant, he retired to a law practice but still yearned for action in the field. New Mexico offered him an opportunity to demonstrate that Grant had been wrong about him.[2]

Despite piercing eyes, thick hair, and a long mustache, Wallace had a softer look, the look of a teacher. The Civil War general was also a writer. After producing one fairly successful novel, he was now working on a major book about a hero from biblical times. The title of the book would be *Ben Hur*.[3]

In September 1878, Wallace took up residence at the governor's house in Santa Fe and went quickly to work. After reading reports from several agents, Wallace decided that New Mexico's law enforcement and judicial systems were not equipped to handle the growing lawlessness. He asked president Hayes to place New Mexico under the control of the United States military. Although the president did not go as far as Wallace asked, he did allow him to use army troops as posses in New Mexico. Army soldiers could now be used to chase down New Mexico's outlaws.[4]

Lew Wallace—governor of New Mexico, ex-Civil War general, and author—tried to help end the Lincoln County War.

Nevertheless, after hearing stories of the killings and the battles, Wallace decided not to seek vengeance against either side. He wanted to end the hostilities between the two warring forces as soon as possible. On November 13, 1878, he wrote to his superiors in Washington, D.C., "I have this day issued a Proclamation, announcing the end of the disturbances, inviting peaceably disposed citizens who have been driven away to return to their homes."[5] In effect, Wallace was calling an end to the war.

With the power of the army behind him, Wallace had decided on a bold move. He would not equip army units to spend months tracking down criminals across New Mexico. Instead, he decided that the threat itself was enough to persuade men to put down their arms as long as they knew they would not be jailed. His proclamation granted "a general pardon for misdemeanors and offenses committed in the said County of Lincoln against the laws of the said Territory in connection with the aforesaid disorders, between the first day of February, 1878, and the date of this proclamation."[6]

Governor Wallace's offer of pardons, however, did not apply to Billy the Kid. Billy was already under previous indictments for the murders of Sheriff Brady and Buckshot Roberts. Nevertheless, Wallace decided to protect the young outlaw from prosecution if he agreed to tell all he knew.[7]

The Kid Talks Peace

Billy told one of his friends in early 1879 that he was tired of running. Deciding to work out a peace settlement between the Regulators and the Dolan men, Billy sent a message asking whether the two sides could discuss laying down arms.

On February 18, one year to the day after John Tunstall had been killed, Billy and other Regulators met in Lincoln with Dolan, Jesse Evans, and other Dolan men. After lengthy talks, the two sides agreed to end the fighting. They even drew up a peace treaty, signed it, and then went to a bar to celebrate. After much drinking and some insults, the crowd of veteran fighters scuffled. Some fired off shots, and one man fell dead. So much for peace treaties![8]

Despite the setback, Billy the Kid decided to approach Wallace. On March 13, 1879, he sent a letter to the governor saying that he had come to Lincoln to make friends with old enemies. If the charges were dropped against him, he said, he would tell all he knew about various aspects of the conflict.[9]

Wallace instructed Billy to meet him alone at a house in downtown Lincoln, near the courthouse. On March 17, Wallace met the young fugitive who had been causing so much commotion. Billy came to the door of the house with a Winchester rifle in one hand and a revolver in the other. When he saw that Wallace had no armed guard with him, he put down his guns and sat down next to the governor in the dimly lit room.[10]

Wallace told Billy that he had the power to pardon him for his crimes if he would provide information about the Lincoln County War. For several days, Billy told the governor and others much of what he knew about various events in the war. But Billy became increasingly nervous about his situation, reluctant to trust Wallace and those around the governor. Billy decided to run. He was once again a fugitive.[11]

On the Outlaw Trail

A desperado running around New Mexico with various outlaws, Billy became an even bigger story for the newspapers and for gossip, from the boardinghouses to the saloons. Rumors about his whereabouts made the rounds throughout the state. People saw him everywhere, or at least they thought they did. Numerous outrages were blamed on Billy that he could not possibly have committed. They blamed him for counterfeit money that was circulating in the West. They blamed him for numerous murders.

The Kid did, however, engage in enough crime to feed his bad reputation. He stole horses. He rustled cattle. The Pecos Valley of New Mexico was a perfect location for cattle rustling. There, large ranches stretched vast distances. In winter, fierce storms drove the scattered herds of cattle to the edges of these ranches, into areas where enterprising thieves could easily round the cattle up, drive them off the ranges, and hide them in herds of their own.

In New Mexico, near the eastern border, is Los Portales, an area of rough rock formations with abundant water. It was there that Billy and other outlaws had their "ranches," hiding cattle until they could sell them off.[12] The chief markets were the government post at Fort Stanton, the Mescalero Apache Indian Agency, and the booming new gold-mining town of White Oaks. Rustling cattle, partying in the saloons and gambling parlors in

Outlaw Rock

About four miles west of Fort Selden in southwestern New Mexico, Billy and other members of his gang, including Charlie Bowdre, Tom O'Folliard, and Dave Rudabaugh, spent time hiding out in an old adobe hut in the mountains overlooking the surrounding area. On a craggy peak, the four apparently carved their initials. The peak became known in the surrounding area as "Outlaw Rock." The initials can still be seen today.

White Oaks and Lincoln, Billy dodged the law. Annie Lesnett, one of the individuals who allowed Billy and his men to hide in her home, had known him since he first moved to Silver City. Lesnett said, "I did give Billy the Kid several meals when he would come to our place. . . . I felt so sorry for them when they said they were hungry."[13]

One old-timer from New Mexico said of Billy: "He was a tough customer, ruthless with his enemies, but generous to his friends . . . his good looks, charming personality, and fine dancing won him the admiration of the younger set . . . but he was a desperado, a gunman and a killer. . . ."[14]

In San Elizario, Texas, near the New Mexico border, stands a jail from which Billy the Kid did not escape. It is, instead, a jail that Billy broke *into*. While in Las Cruces, Billy had learned that a friend had been arrested and was being held in the San Elizario jail. After traveling the fifty miles on horseback, Billy arrived in San Elizario in the middle of the night. When he knocked on the door of the jail, one of the guards inside called out, "Who is it?" Billy answered, "The Texas Rangers. We have two . . . prisoners." When the guard opened the door, he was looking into the face of Billy the Kid and down the barrel of Billy's revolver. Billy relieved the guard of his gun, got the gun of another guard, found the key to the cell, and freed his friend. After locking

Did Billy the Kid Meet Jesse James?
In July 1879, Billy the Kid was in Las Vegas, New Mexico, a popular hangout for criminals, gamblers, and others on the run. According to one of Billy's friends, a man whose stories about Billy have generally proven to be accurate, Jesse James, the notorious bank robber and railroad bandit, was also in town. In the restaurant of a Las Vegas hotel, Billy was introduced to a "Mr. Howard," the alias that Jesse James lived under during those years. Billy himself said later that he had, indeed, met Jesse James. Although the story at first sounds suspiciously like many other fictional accounts of Billy's life, it is entirely possible, considering all the evidence available, that Jesse James was in New Mexico at that time and that the two outlaws did meet.

the two jailers in the cell, the two desperadoes rode across the river into Mexico.[15]

Near White Oaks, nine members of a posse chased Billy to a cave. Hiding behind the rocks at the far end of the cave, Billy held his fire as several of the men walked through the entrance. They did not see him and left. Billy later said that several members of the posse had been his friends. He could have killed several of them, he said, but would have shot them down only if he had been cornered.[16]

In the middle of the night sometime in August 1879, a posse surrounded Billy in a cabin six miles

Billy the Kid spent many days in Fort Sumner, New Mexico.

south of Lincoln. Again, he escaped. He did it the same way he had when he was twelve years old: He climbed out the chimney.[17]

On January 10, 1880, Billy and a group of his friends were drinking in a saloon in Fort Sumner. A man named Joe Grant was making himself particularly obnoxious, especially to Billy. Drunk and staggering across the barroom, Grant began smashing bottles on the bar and promising to shoot someone. He tried to shoot Billy. Unfortunately for Grant, his revolver was half empty, and his next shot would be from one of the gun's empty chambers. As Billy was leaving the saloon, he heard a click from Grant's gun. The Kid calmly turned and killed Joe Grant.[18]

Billy's outlaw activity in New Mexico had reached such a point by late 1880 that state officials knew they needed a determined campaign to bring him down. Elusive, fast on the draw, and intelligent, Billy had become a serious embarrassment to law enforcement authorities and elected state officials. The leaders of the state were ready for a no-nonsense, systematic effort to end the Billy the Kid problem once and for all. They would find the best tracker they could. They would give him the money necessary to do the job, and send him out to destroy what they saw as a menace to society.

8

THE KID
GOES DOWN

To track down Billy the Kid, Lincoln County turned to a lawman named Pat Garrett. Born in Chambers County, Alabama, on June 5, 1850, Pat Garrett was three when his widowed father moved his eight children to an eighteen-hundred-acre plantation in Claiborne Parish, Louisiana. At age eighteen, Garrett left for Texas, where he briefly farmed and ranched. North of Abilene, he struggled for a year as a buffalo hunter. He also worked as a bartender. A skilled marksman, he arrived at Fort Sumner, New Mexico, in 1878 and took a job with rancher Pete Maxwell. The quiet, lanky, six-foot five-inch Garrett was nicknamed *Juan Largo* (Long

John). He fought off American Indian rustlers for some of the local cattlemen and became known as a fierce tracker.[1] He also became acquainted with Billy the Kid.[2]

Garrett was elected Lincoln County sheriff on November 2, 1880. His supporters promised that their law-and-order candidate, this veteran rifleman, would take down Billy the Kid and the other outlaws who continued making a mockery of local law enforcement.

Across central and eastern New Mexico and into the Texas Panhandle, Billy and his gang wandered. They rustled cattle. They engaged in barroom brawls. They got their names into the papers. On a frigid, snowy night in late November, before Pat Garrett had taken over as sheriff, Billy and several of his friends were trapped in a house by a posse led by Deputy James Carlyle. The lawman agreed to meet Billy inside the house to talk over terms of surrender. After the talks broke down, Carlyle was gunned down as he tried to leave. He fell dead in the snow. With the posse shaken by Carlyle's death, Billy and his men charged through the doorway, mounted their horses, and rode off. The posse gave up the fight. Billy had escaped again.[3]

Jim Carlyle was a popular man in Lincoln County, and his death seemed senseless and tragic. Aware that public opinion was against him in the

Pat Garrett—the lawman put on the trail of Billy the Kid.

Carlyle killing, Billy wrote to Governor Wallace denying responsibility not only for Carlyle's killing but for the rustling going on in the community. There was much stealing taking place in New Mexico, said Billy, but he was not one of the thieves.[4]

Wallace did not believe Billy's denials. Instead, in December 1880, the governor offered a reward for the capture of Billy the Kid:

> $500 REWARD—I will pay $500 reward to any person or persons who will capture William Bonney, alias The Kid, and deliver him to any sheriff of New Mexico. Satisfactory proofs of identity will be required. Lew. Wallace, Governor of New Mexico.[5]

The Hunter and the Hunted

In mid-December 1880, Pat Garrett was ready to begin his manhunt. He learned from friends that Billy planned to ride into Fort Sumner on the night of December 19 to attend a private dance. The weather was bitterly cold and snow blanketed the region. Garrett moved his posse into an abandoned soldier's hospital near Fort Sumner where Charlie Bowdre, one of Billy's gang members, was living with his wife. The posse figured that Billy's gang would certainly show up at the hospital. They decided to lay in wait.

Several of the posse members entered the building and began playing poker by the fireplace. The others stayed outside to look for the approach of the

Charlie Bowdre, a friend of Billy the Kid's, posed with his wife.

Kid and his men. At about eight o'clock in the evening, with the moonlight reflecting off the snow, the posse members stationed outside got a good look at several riders approaching the hospital. It was Billy and his gang. Garrett positioned his men at the corners of the building. When the riders came within a few yards of the house, Garrett yelled at the men to throw up their hands. As one of the posse members later said, ". . . at that moment they jerked guns out and the big shooting came off. There was about 40 shots fired."[6]

Billy and the others wheeled their horses around and dashed for safety. Before they were able to escape, one of them fell wounded in the snow. He was Tom O'Folliard, Billy's close friend. Garrett and the posse helped O'Folliard into the room, made him as comfortable as possible, and continued to play poker. For O'Folliard, his game was over. He died that evening.[7]

Billy and the remainder of his gang headed east. In the frigid cold, the gang arrived at a place called Stinking Springs, a small lodging town for cattle drivers and sheepherders. They holed up in an old, dilapidated rock house, probably convinced that Garrett's men would wait until the weather improved to continue their hunt. The determined Garrett did not wait. The horses of the outlaws had marked a very clear path in the snow, and Garrett pushed his posse east on through the night across the glistening landscape. At the rock house, in the early morning hours of December 21, the members of the posse reached their prey. They surrounded the cabin and waited.

One of the men in the posse, Louis Bousman, remembered lying out all night on blankets in the snow, waiting for the outlaws to leave the house.[8] Garrett later said that in the bitter cold, one of the men of the posse had a beard "full of icicles."[9]

Garrett told his men to look for a man wearing a Mexican hat, a broad-brimmed sombrero with a green hat band. The Kid often wore Mexican clothes. "If Billy goes out to feed the horses . . ." said Garrett, "You boys cut down and kill him."[10]

At dawn, one of the outlaws, wearing a large hat, walked out of the house, carrying a feed bag for the horses. Garrett thought he had Billy in his sights and fired. The other posse members also blasted away. Screaming, the man staggered and fell backward into the doorway. Garrett could see that the man was not Billy but Charlie Bowdre. "We thought it was Billy the Kid," said Louis Bousman. "Afterwards Billy hollered and said Bowdre wanted to come out there to us. Pat told him to come ahead and leave his guns in the house."[11]

Inside, Billy shoved a gun into his friend's hand and told him to get revenge. Bowdre was in no condition to use it. With blood streaming from his mouth, he struggled back outside, fell into the arms of one of the posse members, and surrendered to Garrett. He had been shot in three places and died within a few minutes.[12] Despite the extreme cold, the posse continued to surround the house, waiting out Billy and his friends. They stayed all day. At one point, Billy tried to get all of the gang's horses inside the house to prepare for a dash out the door. The posse would have none of it. They shot one of the horses, and it dropped in front of the door. Any plans the gang members may have had about riding mounted horses through the front door were gone. Billy said later,

> If it hadn't been for the dead horse in the doorway I wouldn't be here. I would have ridden out on my bay mare and taken my chances of escaping. But I couldn't ride out over that, for she would have jumped back, and I would have got it in the head.[13]

With the weather turning even colder, with wind whipping up puffs of snow across the fields, local ranchers brought the posse some meat and other food as well as logs to build a fire. They cooked supper. The whole scene outside was too much for Billy and his men, hungry and cold inside the stone house. At sundown, the posse saw a white flag on a stick wave from one of the windows. It was a flag of surrender. Billy and his men had given up.[14] The Kid, Louis Bousman remembered, ". . . said he smelt that bacon frying and he was right hungry."[15]

Garrett had his man. For Billy the Kid and his gang at Stinking Springs, the place with the terrible name had meant terrible events. The posse took Billy and his gang to Fort Sumner for the night. "We kept Billy the Kid and the others in his bunch, put them in a house—under guard until next morning," Bousman said.[16]

The next day, Garrett allowed Billy to visit one of his girlfriends, Dulcinea del Toboso, before leaving for the jail at Las Vegas, New Mexico. The two embraced before one of the posse broke them apart. The Kid was on his way to jail.[17]

The Prisoner

As Billy and his men were brought into Las Vegas, New Mexico, on Sunday, December 27, 1880, the *Gazette* published a midnight extra. Billy the Kid, the

The Winchester Rifle

When Pat Garrett and his posse captured Billy the Kid at Stinking Springs, New Mexico, Garrett took from the gunslinger a Model 1873 Winchester. Garrett carried the rifle with him throughout his career. Produced by the Winchester Company in Connecticut, the Model 1873 was a .44 caliber, fifteen-shot rifle that became very popular in the last part of the nineteenth century. It was later known as the rifle that won the West.

paper reported, had drawn huge crowds. On street corners, in hotels, and in saloons, people talked about nothing but the famous outlaw now in their jail.[18]

One reporter wrote that Billy seemed agreeable and pleasant, nothing like his reputation as a fierce, animal-like killer. Instead, he looked "like a school boy, with the traditional silky fuzz on his upper lip; clear blue eyes, with a roguish snap about them."[19]

The following day, Billy and the other gang members were transported to Santa Fe. He was held there for three months. Billy and some of the other prisoners began to dig a tunnel under one of the beds, using forks, boards, and pieces of bedspring. They were caught. The Santa Fe jailers had managed to do something that most other jailers had failed to do—hold Billy the Kid in custody.[20]

In late March, Billy was transferred to the town of Mesilla, New Mexico, just south of Las Cruces. On April 10, 1881, Billy stood trial for the killing of Lincoln County Sheriff William Brady in the shootout three years earlier. When the jury delivered the verdict of guilty of murder in the first degree, the judge, staring intently at the solemn young man in handcuffs, said, "You are sentenced to be hanged by the neck until you are dead, dead, dead."[21]

On April 16, deputies quietly loaded Billy into a wagon in front of the Mesilla jail. As a precaution against either an attempted lynching or an attempted rescue, authorities had spread word that he would be sent to Lincoln County in the middle of the following week. Instead, on Saturday night, they slipped him out of town under cover of darkness. Seven men rode guard—a deputy United States marshal, a deputy sheriff, and five men specially deputized for the mission to transport Billy the Kid safely. The posse took the three gang members to Lincoln. The Kid, bound in shackles, was placed in the Lincoln County Courthouse, which was to be used as a jail.

Governor Lew Wallace realized that Billy was a popular figure to many of Santa Fe's citizens. "I heard singing and music the other night," he wrote. Groups of singers had gathered around the Lincoln County Courthouse to serenade Billy.[22]

On April 30, 1881, Governor Lew Wallace signed Billy the Kid's death warrant. He commanded the Sheriff of Lincoln County to

> take the said William Bonny, alias Kid, alias William Antrim, from the county jail of the county of Lincoln wherein he is now confined to some safe and convenient place within the said county and there, between the hours of ten o'clock a.m. and three o'clock p.m. of said day, you hang the said William Bonny, alias Kid, alias William Antrim by the neck until he is dead. . . .[23]

Billy's incarceration in the Lincoln County Courthouse set the stage for his dramatic escape and his killing of the two guards, including his tormentor,

Bob Olinger. Billy rode out of Lincoln on Thursday, April 28, 1881. Pat Garrett learned of Billy the Kid's escape the next day. Not until Saturday, April 30, did a one-line telegram from Socorro bring the news to Governor Lew Wallace in Santa Fe. Billy's escape put the governor's death warrant on hold.

There is a legend that Billy, heavily armed during his escape, stopped to stash some of his weapons to lighten the load. According to the tale, he placed two pistols and the cartridge belts in the fork of an oak tree, planning to return later to retrieve them. He never came back. Somewhere in the Capitan Mountains, the story says, there grows an old oak tree with Billy the Kid's guns in its heart.[24]

A New Manhunt

The news of Billy's escape shocked the entire territory. Clever and daring, the Kid had now established his growing reputation as perhaps the most dreaded desperado in the Southwest. For two and a half months, newspapers carried rumors of his whereabouts. Could he have headed for Arizona or Texas? Many individuals thought he had crossed the border to Mexico and intended to stay there indefinitely.

The frustrated Garrett kept trying to obtain the best information possible about the Kid's whereabouts. He got some help from several lawmen from Texas who had offered to help capture the Kid.[25] To several cattlemen in Texas, Billy's rustling activities there had become especially obnoxious.

Garrett heard rumors that the Kid was actually back in the Fort Sumner area, shielded by several Hispanic sheepherders. The rumors turned out to be true. The Kid had not fled to other states or to Mexico; he was hiding right in the midst of his pursuers. Still, Garrett and his men could not find him.[26]

In July, Garrett got the tip he needed. Billy had been seen at a house in Fort Sumner owned by Pete Maxwell, a friend not only of Pat Garrett's but of Billy's. The Kid had once saved the life of a friend of the Maxwells', and they often invited him to their Fort Sumner house. Since his escape from the Lincoln County Courthouse, Billy had used the Maxwell house as one of his many hiding places.[27]

On July 14, 1881, Pat Garrett and two lawmen arrived at the house. They waited in a peach orchard until dark in case some of the townspeople might recognize them and alert the Kid. At about 11:30 P.M., Garrett went to a bedroom in the building where Pete Maxwell was sleeping. His men stayed on the porch outside and waited. In the darkened bedroom, Garrett moved to the edge of bed, woke up the sleeping Maxwell, and asked him about the Kid's whereabouts. He did not have to wait long.

Billy had spent the evening partying at the home of a friend in Fort Sumner. When he arrived at the

Many lawmen were sent after Billy the Kid. These are three lawmen of New Mexico—from left to right, Pat Garrett, James Brent, and John Poe.

Maxwell house, he apparently noticed the two men. Although he did not recognize them, he became suspicious. As he entered the house, he drew his gun and entered the bedroom. In the dim light, he saw Garrett on the bed. It was too late. As Billy yelled in Spanish *"¿Quien es?"* (Who is it?), Garrett fired twice. The young outlaw dropped to the floor, hit by one of the shots just above his heart.[28]

Garrett quickly ran out of the room, unsure whether the Kid had been fatally hit. Garrett and his men waited on the front porch. When they thought they heard a faint noise from Billy, they walked in. Lighting a candle, they could now see Billy on his back, his eyes staring blankly at the ceiling. The notorious outlaw was dead. When asked later why Billy did not shoot immediately on entering the bedroom in the Maxwell house, Garrett said that he thought Billy—for one of the few times in his life—had been caught off guard, had "lost his presence of mind."[29]

The Daily New Mexican, a paper in Santa Fe, reported the news of Billy's death with near glee:

> The city was thrown into a state of excitement yesterday morning by the announcement that Billy the Kid, the man who has been the terror of peaceable people in this territory for years . . . met the fate that he had meted out to others with such fiendish pleasure, frequently without cause and generally in the most brutal manner.[30]

Another New Mexico paper declared, ". . . all mankind rejoices and the newspapers will now have something else to talk about."[31]

After a candlelight vigil attended by some of his friends, Billy was buried in Fort Sumner's cemetery next to his friends Charlie Bowdre and Tom O'Folliard.[32] Some of Billy the Kid's friends muttered that he had been ambushed, shot down in the dark, that he never had a chance. He was twenty-one years old.

Billy's death made news as far away as New York City. "DESPERADO DIES IN WESTERN GUN PLAY," exclaimed the New York *Sun*. The paper called the Kid a "blood thirsty young outlaw."[33]

An artist's depiction of Billy the Kid being shot and killed by Pat Garrett.

In 1902, over twenty years after he gunned down Billy the Kid, Pat Garrett returned to Billy's grave, accompanied by a Chicago author. Amid the dry tumbleweeds and mesquite brush of the desert around Fort Sumner, Garrett located the common plot of Billy, Charlie Bowdre, and Tom O'Folliard. The old lawman picked up his canteen and offered a toast to the three dead outlaws: "Here's to the boys. If there is any other life, I hope they make better use of it than the one I put them out of."[34]

9

THE LEGENDS OF BILLY THE KID

Billy the Kid was not an evil, vicious killer as he is often portrayed. He was also not the noble, heroic figure pictured by others. The real Billy the Kid—Henry McCarty—died ingloriously in a dark bedroom. He was well-known in New Mexico at the time of his death. He was mentioned from time to time in newspapers across the country as a notorious outlaw with a fast draw and a knack for escaping from any jail in which he found himself. At the time of his death, he was a convicted murderer who had missed hanging only because he had again managed to escape. His influence on the Lincoln County War or other historical events in New Mexico or United States history was minimal.

The better-known Billy the Kid never died. That Billy became a far different character from the real Billy. He became what several generations of Americans have wanted him to be, the creation of many writers, songwriters, playwrights, and moviemakers. Through these works, a legend and a towering figure in American folklore was born, and the life of this young drifter in New Mexico over a hundred years ago achieved lasting national significance.

The Final Escape: Believing the Kid Still Lives

Some people over the years refused to accept the fact that Billy the Kid had actually been killed by Pat Garrett on that night in Fort Sumner. Billy thus joined other heroes from many times and places, who, in the eyes of some believers, have seemed to escape death. Many refused to believe that the Russian czar had been killed at the turn of the century. Generations later, some claimed that the rock-and-roll singer Elvis Presley did not actually die as reported and is not buried in a grave in Memphis, Tennessee. Legends are often not allowed to simply perish. For those who refuse to accept all the hard evidence, there must be other explanations.[1]

Several books over the years have tried to explain how Billy managed to escape Pat Garrett's death shot. Some authors concluded that the entire shootout in Maxwell's house was an elaborate hoax set up by Billy himself. In the twentieth century, several men, claiming to be Billy, lugged old six-shooters to lectures and gave personal appearances for money.

Even some of Billy's acquaintances doubted that he had been killed. Ygenio Salazar, a close friend of Billy's, said he had received a letter from Billy many years later, confirming that the shootout had been a hoax. In the 1930s, a priest told of an old man who died in an isolated area of California and asked, as a dying wish, that his friends in New Mexico be informed that he was actually Billy the Kid.[2]

José García y Trujillo, an Hispanic rancher in Albuquerque, New Mexico, argued in an interview that Billy had not died:

> I don't want to dispute against you . . . but in my mind which is the picture of my soul, I know it is not true. Maybe Pat Garrett, he give Billy the Keed money to go to South America and write that story for the looks. Maybe he kill somebody else in Billy's place.[3]

Despite the denials, Billy the Kid almost certainly died that night in Fort Sumner. His legend, nevertheless, lives on.

Glory in the Gunfighter

Billy the gunfighter was a convenient historical figure around whom writers could weave fictional tales. His fast-draw reputation, the many men he had supposedly killed, his daring escapes from numerous jails, and his violent death in Maxwell's bedroom were all part of a dramatic story. Here was enough raw material around which others could invent and add new adventures, characters, and settings.

Many different images of Billy the Kid have showered America over the years, most of them pure nonsense. But we tell the old stories again and again and each time the deeds seem to become even more astonishing, the figures even more romantic. Magazine pieces, plays, motion pictures, verses, pamphlets, fiction—they have all used the figure of Billy the Kid to spin magical tales of the West. Arlo Guthrie, Bob Dylan, and Billy Joel have composed songs about Billy. Zane Grey, O. Henry, and Larry McMurtry have all written stories about him. Aaron Copland produced a ballet about the Kid.

The story of Billy the Kid had one constant theme—death by gunfire. All of the principal characters around Billy, his friends and employers, most of them in their twenties, died by gun: John Tunstall, Alexander McSween, Dick Brewer, Tom O'Folliard, and Charlie Bowdre. Billy's most despised enemies suffered the same fate: Buckshot Roberts, Bob Olinger, Jesse Evans. Even Pat Garrett, who lived well beyond the era of Billy the Kid, died by gunfire, shot in the back near Las Cruces, New Mexico, in 1908 by an unknown assailant.[4]

In New York and other eastern cities, newspapers ran stories about Billy killing twenty-one men—one for each of the twenty-one years of his life—an assertion made by one reporter based on no factual evidence and repeated over and over again. In one obituary, Billy appeared ". . . with fangs snarling and firing a revolver like a maniac."[5]

This atmosphere of violence, this suddenness of extinction by gun, would fascinate Americans through the years. Its drama gave a special meaning to the frontier and life to the legend of Billy the Kid.

Gunfighters and the Western Code

In books, movies, television, and folk songs, gunfighters of the American West are often portrayed as living under a code of honor. Gunfighters dueled in fair fights and never shot anyone in the back, so the code said. In reality, the only trait shared by most gunfighters seems to have been to shoot first. Jesse James was shot in the back in his own home. Wild Bill Hickok was shot in the back while playing poker. Wyatt Earp's brother was shot in the back in a saloon. Billy the Kid was shot as he entered a darkened room. Pat Garrett, the man who shot Billy the Kid, was himself shot in the back of the head along the side of a road.

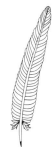

Pat Garrett: Author

Billy's legend was partly manufactured by the man who killed him. Shortly after the Kid's death, Pat Garrett published *The Authentic Life of Billy the Kid, the Noted Desperado of the Southwest, Whose Deeds of Daring and Blood Have Made His Name A Terror in New Mexico, Arizona and Northern Mexico.* The book itself was written by Garrett's old friend, Marshall "Ash" Upson, a newspaperman who had lived for a time with the Garrett family.

Pat Garrett and Ash Upson were anything but "authentic" in presenting the life of the Kid. Intent on making himself appear to be a genuine American hero, Garrett exaggerated the criminal deeds of the man he brought down. In the book, Billy was a vicious killer who had to be exterminated for the good of society. In publishing the error-filled, misleading book, Garrett actually made Billy the Kid into a figure whose criminal deeds took on a mythical character.

In Garrett's stories of Billy, there had never been a boy so young with such evil talents—a lightning-fast gunman, an escape artist of almost magical abilities, a killer with no remorse or guilt. Garrett made Billy into a character of such fascinating proportions that he became irresistible to writers, songwriters, and others looking for subjects to turn into legends. The books, songs, and legends that

followed in later generations would not be about Pat Garrett, as the lawman had undoubtedly hoped; they would be about Billy the Kid.[6]

The Dime Novels

In the 1880s, one of the most popular forms of entertainment for the public was the dime novel. The paperback books were short, inexpensive, and filled with wild tales of adventure. Although some of the dime novels used themes ranging from pirates to children detectives, the most frequently used subjects were the American West and the frontier. There were stories of backwoodsmen, pioneers, and lumberjacks. Especially, there were stories about outlaws and lawmen. The dime novels, published in various sizes and formats, sometimes printing more than one hundred thousand copies at a time, were popular with young readers and working-class audiences for several decades.

In the dime novels, writers produced *Old King Brady and Billy the Kid; Desperado of Apache Land; Daredevil Deeds of Billy the Kid;* and *Buffalo Bill and Billy the Kid.* In some stories, Billy was a murderer, counterfeiter, or kidnapper; in others, he was hanged or shot, and in at least one book, turned his life to the side of the law. For a dime, readers could get Billy the Kid, the boy with the snappy name, the mysterious past, and the fascinating outlaw deeds. It was here in America's cheap thriller book industry that fact and fiction melted together. It was here that the western outlaw hero was first mass-produced.

Hollywood and Billy

Early in the twentieth century, the motion-picture industry gave outlaws a new identity. In the darkness of the theaters, to spirited music, viewers could see *The Great Train Robbery*, the first of the great western films, and others that followed through the years.

In the films, Billy the Kid would be there, large as life, with the excitement and danger of robberies, gunfights, and chases on horseback. There on the screen, moviegoers would begin to experience things about which they had only read. With the creation of motion pictures, the leap from bad man to legend became far easier.

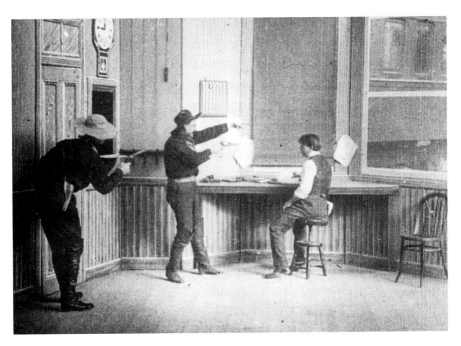

Many Americans later learned about the West and its famous figures such as Billy the Kid through motion pictures. The Great Train Robbery, filmed at the turn of the century, was the first full-length film about the West.

Hollywood has told and retold the story of Billy the Kid since the early days of the movie industry. In 1930, ex-football star Johnny Mack Brown played the lead in the film *Billy the Kid*, directed by King Vidor. It was the first of more than fifty motion pictures produced by Hollywood with Billy the Kid as the central figure.

As in the dime novels, Billy has been portrayed as a romantic hero, as a savage killer, and as a misunderstood loner. In some of the films, he has even been a romantic cowboy who sang love songs to female admirers. In other films, the Kid has been paired with Dracula and Mickey Mouse. Famous directors, including Howard Hughes, Arthur Penn, and Sam Peckinpah, and actors, including Roy Rogers, Audie Murphy, Paul Newman, and Emilio Estevez, have brought to the screen their unique portrayals of the Kid.[7]

Making and Remaking the Image

The wife of one of the members of the posse that captured Billy at Stinking Springs said that Billy's image had been distorted by stories and legends. Although writers had pictured the Kid as a mean man, she said, he was considered brave and loyal by his friends.[8]

The Kid was, indeed, not entirely the cruel killer who notched one victim for each year he lived. Most of the murders attributed to Billy the Kid in the stories and legends handed down for generations were totally fictional. Some were based on rumor and exaggeration; others were invented.

There is, for example, the story that Billy, while a very young teenager in Silver City, killed a Chinese man. It is true that the gang of young toughs that Billy had joined for a brief period in Silver City did kill a Chinese man in a rock-throwing incident. The killing, however, occurred four years after Billy had left Silver City. Local gossip and legend, however, took over, placing Billy at the scene.

When journalists and other writers heard the story of the gang and the Chinese man, the next step was to include Billy in the incident. Then, as the story changed with each retelling, Billy himself became the murderer. As the story took on a life of its own, new "facts" were invented. In the new version, the murder resulted from Billy's sale of a stolen keg of butter to the Chinese man, who betrayed him to the police. Billy gets revenge by slitting the throat of the man and then escaping up a chimney. The chimney part of the story undoubtedly came from Billy's actual escape from jail after he was charged with stealing clothes from a laundry—a Chinese laundry, of course. Billy and the chimney and the Chinese—all of it mixed with fictitious events to create one of many enduring myths about Billy the Kid.[9]

The Saga of Billy the Kid

In the years immediately following Billy's death, the images were distorted mostly against him. In 1926, however, a Chicago newspaperman named Walter Noble Burns wrote a fictional account entitled *The Saga of Billy the Kid.* The book received mass circulation in December 1926 when it was the primary offering for the Book-of-the-Month Club.

With the publication of Burns's book, Billy the Kid became a new and far different figure. From the pen of Burns, Billy became a criminal who did it all for good causes, a gang leader who was the idol of simple Mexican herdsmen of the Southwest. In Burns's book, Billy was not villainous but generous; he was not a vicious killer but a man fighting for principle against unprincipled men. Billy became a new hero, a Robin Hood whose evil deeds came from noble motives.

Because it became an overnight best-seller, Walter Burns's book, more than any other, established the Kid as a noble figure. From Burns's book, authors, poets, songwriters, playwrights, moviemakers, and others drew inspiration.[10]

Comic Books

In the 1950s, Billy the Kid became a familiar but confusing character in children's comic books. In some of the comics, he was the familiar bandit with a heart; in others, he was simply a juvenile delinquent.

In 1969, one comic book series presented the Kid as an eighty-three-year-old hero who returned to the West to fight for noble causes. The Kid battled machine guns, air-to-ground rockets, and jet fighters.[11]

Television

In the early 1950s, television introduced to millions of American homes numerous series and productions on the American West. Billy the Kid appeared sometimes as a central figure, and often as a minor character. Frequently, his name was merely mentioned as a legendary gunslinger. In 1960, NBC television presented *The Tall Man*, a series starring Clu Gulager as the Kid and Barry Sullivan as Pat Garrett. Paul Newman starred in Gore Vidal's play about the death of Billy the Kid.[12]

The Kid Lives

Much of American history is filled with figures who satisfy the public's appetite for excitement and color, for violence and daring. Billy the Kid, as a bandit hero, gives the public an action figure—a tough, courageous fighter who wins against long odds. As this kind of model, Billy the Kid endures.

And so, in books and on the screen, Billy continues to charge from one adventure to another, as both a hero and a villain. The image of this young ruffian in frontier New Mexico becomes what any writer, television producer, or moviemaker wants him to be. From novels to works of music, history, and literature, Billy's story gets forever larger. The Kid rides on.

CHRONOLOGY

1859—Henry McCarty born (estimate).

1873—*March 1*: Catherine McCarty marries William Antrim in Santa Fe, New Mexico.

1874—*September 16*: Catherine McCarty dies.

1875—*September 23*: Henry McCarty is arrested in Silver City for stealing clothes.

1877—*August 17*: "Kid Antrim" kills "Windy" Cahill.

Fall: "William Bonney" arrives in Lincoln County, New Mexico.

1878—*January*: William Bonney hired as cowboy by John H. Tunstall and Alexander McSween.

February 18: Tunstall killed by men working for Lawrence G. Murphy and J. J. Dolan.

February: Pro-Tunstall workers form a small army called "The Regulators."

March 9: Regulators kill three Murphy-Dolan men.

April 1: Regulators kill Sheriff William Brady and one of his deputies in Lincoln.

April 4: Regulators kill Andrew "Buckshot" Roberts, a Murphy-Dolan man, at Blazer's Mill, New Mexico.

April 18: Billy the Kid and others are indicted for the murder of Brady.

July 15–19: Regulators and Murphy-Dolan forces battle in Lincoln; McSween killed.

September 4: President Rutherford B. Hayes appoints General Lew Wallace governor of New Mexico Territory.

1879—Billy makes living stealing horses and gambling.
–1880

1880—*November 2*: Pat Garrett is elected sheriff.

December 1: Billy and several of his friends battle a posse under Deputy James Carlyle; Carlyle is killed.

December 13: Governor Wallace offers reward for capture of Billy.

December 18: Tom O'Folliard, ally of Billy, is killed by Pat Garrett's posse.

December 24: Garrett captures Billy at Stinking Springs, New Mexico.

1881—*April 10–15*: Court in Mesilla, New Mexico, convicts Billy of murder; He is sentenced to hang.

April 28: Billy escapes from Lincoln County Courthouse.

July 14: Garrett kills Billy in Maxwell house at Fort Sumner, New Mexico.

1908—*February 28*: Pat Garrett is shot to death.

CHAPTER NOTES

Chapter 1. The Kid Escapes

1. Alan Lomax, *The Folk Songs of North America* (New York: Doubleday & Company, 1975), p. 387.

2. Robert M. Utley, *Billy the Kid: A Short and Violent Life* (Lincoln: University of Nebraska Press, 1989), p. 177.

3. Pat Garrett, *The Authentic Life of Billy the Kid* (Norman: University of Oklahoma Press, 1954), p. 134.

4. Walter Noble Burns, *The Saga of Billy the Kid* (New York: Doubleday, 1926), p. 233.

5. WPA Life Histories Collection, Library of Congress, Berta Ballard Manning, February 6, 1937.

6. WPA Life Histories Collection, Library of Congress, Mrs. A. E. Lesnett, September 30, 1937.

7. Jay Robert Nash, *Bloodletters and Bad Men* (New York: Warner Books, 1975), p. 51.

8. Jon Tuska, *Billy the Kid: A Handbook* (Lincoln: University of Nebraska Press, 1983), pp. 96–98; Stephen Tatum, *Inventing Billy the Kid: Visions of the Outlaw in America, 1881–1981* (Albuquerque: University of New Mexico Press, 1982), p. 33.

9. WPA Life Histories Collection, Library of Congress, Amelia Bolton Church, September 23, 1938.

10. WPA Life Histories Collection, Library of Congress, Louis Bousman, September 7, 1934.

11. Ramon A. Adams, *Burrs Under the Saddle: A Second Look at Books and Histories of the West* (Norman: University of Oklahoma Press, 1964), p. 29.

12. *The Gunfighters* (Alexandria, Va.: Time-Life Books, 1974), p. 190.

13. WPA Life Histories Collection, Library of Congress, Mrs. J. P. Church, January 22, 1937; Amelia Bolton Church, September 23, 1938; Louis Bousman, September 7, 1934.

14. WPA Life Histories Collection, Library of Congress, Daniel Carabajal, January 20, 1939.

15. WPA Life Histories Collection, Library of Congress, Carolatta Baca Brent, January 1, 1938.

16. WPA Life Histories Collection, Library of Congress, Sam Farmer, July 25, 1938.

17. WPA Life Histories Collection, Library of Congress, Mrs. Amelia Bolton Church, September 23, 1938.

Chapter 2. Who Was the Kid?

1. Don Cline, *Antrim and Billy* (College Station, Tex.: Creative Publishing Company, 1990), p. 44; Kent Steckmesser, *The Western Hero in History and Legend* (Norman: University of Oklahoma Press, 1965), p. 58.

2. Philip Rasch, *Trailing Billy the Kid* (Laramie, Wyo.: National Association for Outlaw and Lawman History, Inc., 1995), p. 10.

3. Robert M. Utley, *High Noon in Lincoln: Violence on the Western Frontier* (Lincoln: University of Nebraska Press, 1987), p. 3.

4. Rasch, p. 15.

5. Joel Jacobsen, *Such Men as Billy the Kid* (Lincoln: University of Nebraska Press, 1994), p. 14.

6. Jerry Weddle, *Antrim Is My Stepfather's Name: The Boyhood of Billy the Kid* (Tucson: Arizona Historical Society, 1993), pp. 7–8.

7. *The Gunfighters* (Alexandria, Va.: Time-Life Books, 1974, p. 183.

8. Weddle, p. 17.

9. Lee Priestley, *Billy the Kid: The Good Side of a Bad Man* (Las Cruces, N.M.: Yucca Tree Press, 1993), p. 12.

10. Weddle, p. 19.

11. WPA Life Histories Collection, Library of Congress, George Bede, no date.

12. Priestley, pp. 10–11.

13. WPA Life Histories Collection, Library of Congress, Mrs. Louis Abraham, November 2, 1937.

14. Utley, p. 3.

15. Weddle, pp. 9, 22–23.

16. Jon Lewis, *The Mammoth Book of the West: The Making of the American West* (New York: Carroll & Graf Publishers, Inc., 1996), p. 208.

17. Joseph, G. Rosa, *The Gunfighter: Man or Myth?* (Norman: University of Oklahoma Press, 1969), p. 46.

18. Cline, p. 68.

19. Robert, F. Kadlec, ed., *They "Knew" Billy the Kid: Interviews with Old-Time New Mexicans* (Santa Fe, N.M.: Ancient City Press, 1987), p. 7.

20. Stephen Tatum, *Inventing Billy the Kid: Visions of the Outlaw in America, 1881–1981* (Albuquerque: University of New Mexico Press, 1982), p. 19.

21. Jon Tusca, *Billy the Kid: A Handbook* (Lincoln: University of Nebraska Press, 1983), p. 55.

Chapter 3: The Kid Notches His First

1. Joseph G. Rosa, *The Gunfighter: Man or Myth?* (Norman: University of Oklahoma Press, 1969), pp. 70–71.

2. Philip Rasch, *Training Billy the Kid* (Laramie, Wyo.: National Association for Outlaw and Lawman History, Inc., 1995), p. 189.

3. Jon Tusca, *Billy the Kid: A Handbook* (Lincoln: University of Nebraska Press, 1983), p. 6.

4. Jerry Weddle, "Apprenticeship of an Outlaw: 'Billy the Kid' in Arizona," *The Journal of Arizona History*, Autumn 1990, p. 236.

5. Don Cline, *Antrim and Billy* (College Station, Tex.: Creative Publishing Company, 1990), p. 68.

6. Weddle, p. 245.

7. Jon Lewis, *The Mammoth Book of the West: The Making of the American West* (New York: Carroll & Graf Publishers, Inc., 1996), p. 209.

8. Ibid.

9. WPA Life Histories Collection, Library of Congress, Lorencita Miranda, May 5, 1939.

10. WPA Life Histories Collection, Library of Congress, José García y Trujillo, September 26, 1936.

11. Jerry Weddle, *Antrim Is My Stepfather's Name: The Boyhood of Billy the Kid* (Tucson: Arizona Historical Society, 1993), p. 34.

12. *The Gunfighters* (Alexandria, Va.: Time-Life Books, 1974), p. 183.

13. Lee Priestley, *Billy the Kid: The Good Side of a Bad Man* (Las Cruces, N.M.: Yucca Tree Press, 1993), p. 20.

14. Tusca, pp. 6–7.

15. Robert, F. Kadlec, ed., *They "Knew" Billy the Kid: Interviews with Old-Time New Mexicans* (Santa Fe, N.M.: Ancient City Press, 1987), p. 12.

16. Eve Ball, *Ma'm Jones of the Pecos* (Tucson: University of Arizona Press, 1969), pp. 117–121.

17. Weddle, "Apprenticeship of an Outlaw: 'Billy the Kid' in Arizona," p. 248.

Chapter 4: A War Brewing in Lincoln County

1. Frederick Nolan, *The Lincoln County War: A Documentary History* (Norman: University of Oklahoma Press, 1992), pp. 36–43.

2. WPA Life Histories Collection, Library of Congress, Mrs. Lorencita Miranda, May 5, 1939.

3. Jon Lewis, *The Mammoth Book of the West: The Making of the American West* (New York: Carroll & Graf Publishers, Inc., 1996), p. 210.

4. Philip Rasch, *Trailing Billy the Kid* (Laramie, Wyo.: National Association for Outlaw and Lawman History, Inc., 1995), p. 21.

5. WPA Life Histories Collection, Library of Congress, Louis Bousman, September 7, 1934.

6. Warren Beck, *New Mexico: A History of Four Centuries* (Norman: University of Oklahoma Press, 1962), pp. 163–165.

7. Joel Jacobsen, *Such Men as Billy the Kid: The Lincoln County War Reconsidered* (Lincoln: University of Nebraska Press, 1987), pp. 18–19.

8. Robert Utley, *High Noon in Lincoln: Violence on the Western Frontier* (Albuquerque: University of New Mexico Press, 1987), p. 12.

9. Frazier Hunt, *The Tragic Days of Billy the Kid* (New York: Hastings House, 1956), p. 21.

10. Leon C. Metz, *The Shooters* (New York: Berkley Books, 1976), p. 20.

11. Walter Noble Burns, *The Saga of Billy the Kid* (New York, Doubleday, 1926), pp. 27–30

12. Robert M. Utley, *Billy the Kid: A Short and Violent Life* (Lincoln: University of Nebraska Press, 1989), p. 37.

13. Utley, *High Noon*, p. 16.

14. Nolan, pp. 155–157, 505.

15. Leon C. Metz, *Pat Garrett: The Story of a Western Lawman* (Norman: University of Oklahoma Press, 1974), p. 47.

16. WPA Life Histories Collection, Library of Congress, Berta Ballard Manning, February 6, 1937.

17. WPA Life Histories Collection, Library of Congress, Amelia Bolton Church, October 3, 1938.

Chapter 5: The Regulators

1. Harold L. Edwards, *Goodbye Billy the Kid* (College Station, Tex.: Creative Publishing Company, 1995), p. 26.

2. Walter Noble Burns, *The Saga of Billy the Kid* (New York: Doubleday, 1926), pp. 105–106.

3. WPA Life Histories Collection, Library of Congress, Amelia Bolton Church, September 23, 1938.

4. Donald Cline, *Alias Billy the Kid: The Man Behind the Legend* (Santa Fe, N.M.: Sunstone Press, 1986), p. 67.

5. Joseph G. Rosa, *The Gunfighter: Man or Myth?* (Norman: University of Oklahoma Press, 1989), pp. 184–186.

6. WPA Life Histories Collection, Library of Congress, Mrs. A. E. Lesnett, September 7, 1938.

7. Robert M. Utley, *Billy the Kid: A Short and Violent Life* (Lincoln: University of Nebraska Press, 1989), p. 72.

8. Dale Walker, *Great Mysteries of the American West* (New York: Tom Doherty Associates, 1997), p. 117.

9. WPA Life Histories Collection, Library of Congress, Francisco Gomez, August 15, 1938.

10. WPA Life Histories Collection, Library of Congress, José Montoya, December 27, 1937.

11. Lee Priestley, *Billy the Kid: The Good Side of a Bad Man* (Las Cruces, N.M.: Yucca Tree Press, 1993), p. 35.

12. Robert, F. Kadlec, ed., *They "Knew" Billy the Kid: Interviews with Old-Time New Mexicans* (Santa Fe, N.M.: Ancient City Press, 1987), p. 80.

13. Cline, p. 87.

14. Walter Noble Burns, *The Saga of Billy the Kid* (New York: Grosset and Dunlap, 1926), p. 185.

15. Cline, pp. 87–88.

16. WPA Life Histories Collection, Library of Congress, Mrs. A. E. Lesnett, September 30, 1937.

17. WPA Life Histories Collection, Library of Congress, Francisco Gomez, August 15, 1938.

18. WPA Life Histories Collection, Library of Congress, George Bede, n.d.

19. WPA Life Histories Collection, Library of Congress, Charles L. Ballard, September 16, 1938.

20. Joel Jacobsen, *Such Men as Billy the Kid* (Lincoln: University of Nebraska Press, 1994), p. 125.

21. WPA Life Histories Collection, Library of Congress, Mrs. A. E. Lesnett, September 30, 1937.

Chapter 6: The Battle of Lincoln

1. Joel Jacobsen, *Such Men as Billy the Kid* (Lincoln: University of Nebraska Press, 1994), pp. 173–180.

2. Dale Walker, *Legends and Lies: Great Mysteries of the American West* (New York: Tom Doherty Associates, 1997), p. 118.

3. Jacobsen, p. 184.

4. WPA Life Histories Collection, Library of Congress, Mrs. A. E. Lesnett, September 30, 1937; Ella Davidson, February 18, 1938.

5. WPA Life Histories Collection, Library of Congress, Mrs. A. E. Lesnett, September 30, 1937.

6. Ibid.

7. WPA Life Histories Collection, Library of Congress, Ella Davidon, February 18, 1938.

8. Pat Garrett, *The Authentic Life of Billy the Kid* (Norman: University of Oklahoma Press, 1954), pp. 75–76.

9. Harold L. Edwards, *Goodbye Billy the Kid* (College Station, Tex.: Creative Publishing Company, 1995), p. 38.

10. Frederick Nolan, *The Lincoln County War: A Documentary History* (Norman: University of Oklahoma Press, 1992), p. 564.

11. WPA Life Histories Collection, Library of Congress, Lorencita Miranda, May 5, 1939.

12. WPA Life Histories Collection, Library of Congress, Ella Davidon, February 18, 1938.

13. Robert Utley, *High Noon in Lincoln: Violence on the Western Frontier* (Albuquerque: University of New Mexico Press, 1987), pp. 114–116.

Chapter 7: Runnin' and Rustlin'

1. Frederick S. Calhoun, *The Lawmen: United States Marshals and Their Deputies, 1789–1989* (New York: Penguin Books, 1991), p. 151.

2. Robert M. Utley, *High Noon in Lincoln: Violence on the Western Frontier* (Albuquerque: University of New Mexico Press, 1987), pp. 119–120.

3. *The Gunfighters* (Alexandria, Va.: Time-Life Books, 1974), p. 189.

4. Walter Noble Burns, *The Saga of Billy the Kid* (New York: Doubleday, 1926), pp. 150–151.

5. National Archives, Record Group 48, Records of the Department of the Interior, Letters Received, 1851–1907, Lew Wallace to Carl Schurz, November 13, 1878 (microfilm #M364, roll 8).

6. Frederick Nolan, *The Lincoln County War: A Documentary History* (Norman: University of Oklahoma Press, 1992), p. 358.

7. Leon C. Metz, *The Shooters* (New York: Berkley Books, 1976), p. 23.

8. Utley, *High Noon*, pp. 132–133.

9. Joel Jacobsen, *Such Men as Billy the Kid* (Lincoln: University of Nebraska Press, 1994), pp. 210–211.

10. Dale Walker, *Legends and Lies: Great Mysteries of the American West* (New York: Tom Doherty Associates, 1997), p. 119.

11. WPA Life Histories Collection, Library of Congress, J. Vernon Smithson, May 11, 1936.

12. Robert M. Utley, *Billy the Kid: A Short and Violent Life* (Lincoln: University of Nebraska Press, 1989), p. 129.

13. WPA Life Histories Collection, Library of Congress, Mrs. E. Lesnett, September 7, 1938.

14. WPA Life Histories Collection, Library of Congress, Cruz Alvarez, n.d.

15. "The San Elizario Jail," *San Elizario Independent School District*, <http://dsl.san-elizario.K12.tx.us/history.html>, (July 19, 1999).

16. WPA Life Histories Collection, Library of Congress, J. Y. Thornton, May 27, 1938.

17. Stephen Tatum, *Inventing Billy the Kid: Visions of the Outlaw in America, 1881–1981* (Albuquerque: University of New Mexico Press, 1982), p. 29.

18. Jacobsen, p. 218.

Chapter 8: The Kid Goes Down

1. Leon C. Metz, *Pat Garrett: The Story of a Western Lawman* (Norman: University of Oklahoma Press, 1974), pp. 55–57; Leon C. Metz, *The Shooters* (New York: Berkely Books, 1976), pp. 131–135.

2. Kent Steckmesser, *The Western Hero in History and Legend* (Norman: University of Oklahoma Press, 1965), pp. 67–68.

3. Richard Patterson, *Historical Atlas of the Outlaw West* (Boulder, Colo.: Johnson Books, 1985), p. 117; Metz, *Pat Garrett*, p. 70; Steckmesser, p. 67.

4. Metz, *Pat Garrett*, p. 71. .

5. Frederick Nolan, *The Lincoln County War: A Documentary History* (Norman: University of Oklahoma Press, 1992), p. 401.

6. Cal Polk's testimony in James Earle, ed., *The Capture of Billy the Kid* (College Station, Tex.: Creative Publishing Company, 1988), p. 26.

7. Harold Edwards, *Goodbye Billy the Kid* (College Station, Tex.: Creative Publishing Company, 1995), p. 44; Jim East's testimony in Robert M. Utley, *Billy the Kid: A Short and Violent Life* (Lincoln: University of Nebraska Press, 1989), p. 156.

8. WPA Life Histories Collection, Library of Congress, Louis Bousman, September 7, 1934.

9. Earle, p. 104.

10. WPA Life Histories Collection, Library of Congress, Louis Bousman, September 7, 1934.

11. Ibid.

12. Patterson, p. 124.

13. Earle, p. 144.

14. Ibid., p. 31.

15. WPA Life Histories Collection, Library of Congress, Louis Bousman, September 7, 1934.

16. Ibid.

17. Earle, p. 88.

18. Ibid., p. 120.

19. W. C. Jameson, *The Return of the Outlaw Billy the Kid* (Plano, Tex.: Republic of Texas Press, 1998), p. 131; Steckmesser, p. 68.

20. Metz, *Pat Garrett*, p. 86.

21. Jon Lewis, *The Mammoth Book of the West: The Making of the American West* (New York: Carroll & Graf Publishers, Inc., 1996), p. 219.

22. Lee Priestley, *Billy the Kid: The Good Side of a Bad Man* (Las Cruces, N.M.: Yucca Tree Press, 1993), p. 46.

23. National Archives, Record Group 48, Records of the Department of the Interior, Territorial Papers, New Mexico (microfilm #M364, roll 1).

24. Joann Mazzio, "On the Trail of Billy the Kid," *Southern New Mexico Online Magazine*, <http://www.zianet.com/SNM/billykid.htm>, (July 19, 1999).

25. Metz, *Pat Garrett*, p. 97.

26. Pat Garrett, *The Authentic Life of Billy the Kid* (Norman: University of Oklahoma Press, 1954), p. 142.

27. WPA Life Histories Collection, Library of Congress, José García y Trujillo, August 26, 1936.

28. Garrett, p. 147.

29. Ibid., p. 148.

30. Edwards, p. 66.

31. Stephen Tatum, *Inventing Billy the Kid: Visions of the Outlaw in America, 1881–1981* (Albuquerque: University of New Mexico Press, 1982), p. 37.

32. Patterson, p. 118.

33. *The American Frontier: Opposing Viewpoints* (San Diego: Greenhaven Press, 1994), p. 234.

34. Metz, *Pat Garrett*, p. 126.

Chapter 9: The Legends of Billy the Kid

1. Blaine Harden, "Wanted," *The Washington Post Magazine*, November 19, 1995, p. 26.

2. Richard Patterson, *Historical Atlas of the Outlaw West* (Boulder, Colo.: Johnson books, 1985), p. 118.

3. WPA Life Histories Collection, Library of Congress, José García y Trujillo, August 26, 1936.

4. Leon C. Metz, "Strange Death of Pat Garrett," *Wild West*, February 1998, p. 38.

5. Stephen Tatum, *Inventing Billy the Kid: Visions of the Outlaw in America, 1881–1981* (Albuquerque: University of New Mexico Press, 1982), p. 38.

6. *The Gunfighters* (Alexandria, Va.: Time-Life Books, 1974), p. 192.

7. Tatum, p. 8.

8. WPA Life Histories Collection, Library of Congress, Carolatta Baca Brent, January 1, 1938.

9. Jerry Weddle, *Antrim Is My Stepfather's Name: The Boyhood of Billy the Kid* (Tucson: University of Arizona Historical Society, 1993), p. 57.

10. Leon C. Metz, *Pat Garrett: The Story of a Western Lawman* (Norman: University of Oklahoma Press, 1974), p. 307.

11. Tatum, p. 6.

12. Ibid.

GLOSSARY

adobe—A brick made of earth or clay and straw and dried in the sun.

bad man—A tough guy, a ruffian, a gunman, a killer.

buckshot—A shotgun load of large balls.

cattleman—Owner of a cattle ranch.

Colt—Six-shooter revolving pistol made by Samuel Colt; the West's most popular pistol in the nineteenth century.

cowboy—Man who tends cattle.

deputy—Someone who acts in place of a law enforcement officer.

dime novel—Short piece of adventure fiction published in the latter half of the nineteenth century and the early twentieth century.

monte—A gambling game played with cards and popular in the West of the nineteenth century.

posse—A group of riders brought together, often by a law officer, to track down an outlaw.

ranch—An establishment where livestock is raised.

revolver—A handgun capable of shooting repeatedly.

rustler—A cow thief.

sheriff—Elected law enforcement officer of a county.

six-shooter—The most common term for a revolver.

Smith & Wesson—A pistol invented by gunsmiths Horace Smith and Daniel Wesson and made in Springfield, Massachusetts.

torreón—In the Southwest, a lookout spot, such as a hill or a tower.

FURTHER READING

Books

Breihan, Carl W. *Lawmen and Robbers*. Caldwell, Idaho: The Caxton Printers, Ltd., 1986.

Cline, Donald. *Antrim and Billy*. College Station, Tex.: Creative Publishing Company, 1990.

Earle, James H., ed. *The Capture of Billy the Kid*. College Station, Tex.: Creative Publishing Company, 1988.

Edwards, Harold L. *Goodbye Billy the Kid*. College Station, Tex.: Creative Publishing Company, 1995.

Jacobsen, Joel. *Such Men as Billy the Kid: The Lincoln County War Reconsidered*. Lincoln: The University of Nebraska Press, 1994.

Kadlec, Robert F., ed. *They "Knew" Billy the Kid: Interviews with Old-Time New Mexicans*. Santa Fe, N.M.: Ancient City Press, 1987.

Lewis, Jon. *The Mammoth Book of the West: The Making of the American West*. New York: Carroll & Graf Publishers, Inc., 1996.

Rasch, Philip. *Trailing Billy the Kid*. Laramie, Wyo.: National Association for Outlaw and Lawman History, Inc., 1995.

Slotkin, Richard. *Gunfighter Nation: The Myth of the Frontier in Twentieth Century America*. New York: HarperPerennial, 1992.

Utley, Robert M. *Billy the Kid: A Short and Violent Life*. Lincoln: University of Nebraska Press, 1989.

Internet Addresses

A&E. *Biography.com.* <http://www.biography.com/search/article.jsp?aid=9219349&search=>.

Billy the Kid. November 1, 1998. <http://www.geocities.com/Athens/Styx/9560/index.htm>.

"Sound of the Guns." Crime Library. 2004. <http://www.crimelibrary.com/americana/kid/2.htm>.

Scribe's Tribute to Billy the Kid. n.d. <http://www.outlawscribe.com/Billy_the_Kid.html>.

INDEX